ASIAN SELF-E

Policy Studies Institute (PSI) is one of Europe's leading independent research organisations undertaking studies of economic, industrial and social policy and the workings of political institutions.

PSI is a registered charity, run on a non-profit basis, and is not associated with any political party, pressure group or commercial interest.

PSI attaches great importance to covering a wide range of subject areas with its multidisciplinary approach. The Institute's researchers are organised in groups which currently cover the following programmes:

Crime, Justice and Youth Studies – *Employment* – *Ethnic Equality and Diversity* – *Family Finances* – *Information and Citizenship* – *Information and Cultural Studies* – *Social Care and Health Studies* – *Work, Benefits and Social Participation*

This publication arises from the Ethnic Equality and Diversity Group and is one of over 30 publications made available by the Institute each year.

Information about the work of PSI and a catalogue of publications can be obtained from:
Publications Department, Policy Studies Institute, 100 Park Village East, London NW1 3SR

ASIAN SELF-EMPLOYMENT

The interaction of culture and economics in England

Hilary Metcalf, Tariq Modood and Satnam Virdee

ECONOMIC
BELIEFS AND
BEHAVIOUR

POLICY STUDIES INSTITUTE

The publishing imprint of the independent
POLICY STUDIES INSTITUTE
100 Park Village East, London NW1 3SR
Tel. 0171 468 0468   Fax. 0171 388 0914

ISBN 0 85374 698 2
PSI Report 824

PSI publications are available from:
BEBC Distribution Ltd, P O Box 1496, Poole, Dorset BH12 3YD

Books will normally be dispatched within 24 hours. Cheques should be made payable to BEBC Distribution Ltd.

Credit cards and telephone/fax orders may be placed on the following freephone numbers:
FREEPHONE   0800 262260
FREEFAX   0800 262266

Booktrade representation (UK and Eire):
Broadcast Books, 24 De Montfort Road, London SW16 1LZ
Tel. 0181 677 5129

PSI subscriptions are available from PSI's subscription agent:
Carfax Publishing Company Ltd,
P O Box 25, Abingdon, Oxford OX14 3UE

Laserset by Policy Studies Institute
Printed in Great Britain by Redwood Books, Trowbridge, Wiltshire

CONTENTS

ACKNOWLEDGEMENTS

We are grateful to the Economic and Social Research Council for the generous funding of this project under the Economic Beliefs and Behaviour Programme (award no L122251020). One of the benefits of being part of a Programme is the support one receives, and so we are pleased to be able to thank the other Programme participants. In particular, we would like to thank the Programme Director, Professor Taylor-Gooby for his support and advice at various stages of the project, and for his written comments on an earlier version of Chapter 7; and to Trevor Jones of Liverpool John Moores University for his conference discussion of an earlier version of Chapter 1.

We are very conscious that without the selfless participation of the interviewees we would not have a study at all. So, to them we give a very big 'thank you'. We hope that this study, by publicising the struggles and achievements of self-employed Asians, may be seen as a worthwhile return for the time and information the interviewees gave us. We would also like to thank Patten Smith and Alison Findlay at Social and Community Planning Research (SCPR) for their assistance with the survey design and for organising the fieldwork. Our thanks, too, go to all the interviewers.

Finally, we would like to thank colleagues at PSI. In particular, thanks to James Nazroo for his help with data management, and to Siân Putnam, Karin Erskine and Amanda Trafford for preparing the text for publication.

Chapter 1

RESEARCHING ASIAN SELF-EMPLOYMENT

The growth in South Asian self-employment has been a notable feature of many British urban economies of the last two decades. Research undertaken by the Policy Studies Institute showed that South Asian self-employment took off in the second half of the 1970s (Smith, 1977; Brown, 1984). The Second National Survey of Ethnic Minorities carried out by PSI in 1974 showed that South Asians were less likely to be in self-employment than whites: among white men, the self-employed accounted for 12 per cent of the working population compared to only 8 per cent of South Asian working men (Smith, 1977:92). On the other hand, the Third National Survey of Ethnic Minorities carried out in 1982 found that the intervening period of eight years had witnessed a substantial growth in South Asian businesses in Britain. Brown (1984: 165) found that by 1982 18 per cent of Asian men were in self-employment compared to 14 per cent of white men. This growth in self-employment among Asians has continued throughout the 1980s and into the 1990s (Modood et al, 1997), so that about 100,000 South Asians are now self-employed (Owen, 1993:5).

However, participation in self-employment has been uneven across groups whose origins lie in the Indian sub-continent. Combining Labour Force Survey (LFS) data from 1988-1990, Jones found that about one in seven of Indians and African Asians were self-employed compared to about one in ten Pakistanis and one in 14 Bangladeshis (Jones, 1993:65). This difference is smaller but still apparent for economically active men:

the Fourth National Survey (1994) shows one in four Indians and African Asians men to be self-employed compared with one in five Pakistanis and one in ten Bangladeshis (Modood et al, 1997). A central aim of this book is to help understand this diversity.

In recent years it has become increasingly clear that ethnic minority groups have divergent socio-economic profiles, let alone cultural variations (Modood, 1991). The main data sources are consistent in suggesting that some minority groups such as the African Asians and the Chinese have a much more advantaged educational and economic profile than groups such as the Pakistanis, Bangladeshis and African Caribbeans (Jones, 1993; Peach, 1996; Modood et al, 1997). To what extent these differences are due to economic, cultural or other factors is a matter of current debate. Self-employment is a focus of these debates, for on the one hand it is clearly related to structural factors (Asian self-employment took off at a time of high unemployment), and on the other to ethnicity, in that it is to be found more among some groups than others.

Existing research on ethnic minority self-employment is characterised by a competition between perspectives as well as the possibility of fruitfully combining approaches which emphasise exclusionary economic structures and those which emphasise minority cultures. Moreover, while existing research has paid much attention to why people enter into self-employment, differences between ethnic groups in rates of entry into self-employment, and of business success in particular, have largely been neglected.

This book starts to address these omissions. Using data from a recent survey of self-employed South Asians, it explores the roles of culture, racism and economics in shaping self-employment. The influence of family, religion, education and employment experience are some of the factors which are examined. The different roles of culture, racism and economics in shaping the self-employment experience of Indians, Pakistanis and African Asians are highlighted. The study also links the nature of entry into self-employment with later development and success. The definition of success itself is explored in order to set business success within its cultural context.

ASIAN SELF-EMPLOYMENT AS A RESPONSE TO 'BLOCKED UPWARD MOBILITY'

The first major study in Britain to look at Asian business development, involving 600 small retailers in Bradford, Leicester and the London Borough of Ealing, was carried out in 1978 (Aldrich et al, 1981; McEvoy et al, 1982; Aldrich et al, 1984). In each area, interviews were held at 100 Asian and 100 white businesses. Two important conclusions emerged. One concerned the motives for entry into self-employment of Asians (the 'blocked upward mobility' thesis), and the other was about the prospect of success of their economic endeavours (the 'economic dead-end' thesis).

The study found that one of the major explanations of Asian entry into self-employment was the desire to avoid racial discrimination and the resulting confinement to low status jobs in the labour market (Aldrich et al, 1981:175). The key factor used by Aldrich et al in this explanation was the existence of a relatively large number of well-qualified Asian shopkeepers compared to the more poorly-educated white shopkeepers in their sample. Specifically, Aldrich et al (1981: 177) found that 20 per cent of Asian owners in their sample were graduates compared to only 3 per cent of their white sample.

Two of the main researchers on the above study carried out a further study in 1990-91 which also examined the motives for Asian entry into self-employment (Jones et al, 1994). This study was an interview survey of over 400 owners of small businesses comprising 178 Asian owners, 54 African Caribbean owners and 171 whites. The study was undertaken in 15 widely-spread small localities throughout England.

The researchers found that over a quarter of their Asian respondents gave 'push' factors such as unemployment, underemployment, job dissatisfaction and/or blocked opportunities as their principal business entry motive (Jones et al, 1994: 186). Jones et al concluded that racism in the wider labour market is the primary factor in pushing some members of ethnic minorities into self-employment. Hence, their entry into self-employment is seen as a 'damage limitation' exercise to avoid unemployment and low status work (Jones et al, 1994).

Further evidence to support this view is provided by Ram (1992). He examined the market and managerial settings of Asian employers in a typical inner-city area of Wolverhampton in the West Midlands. The study did not concentrate on the corner shop but rather on Asian employers in clothing, engineering, professional services as well as retail. He interviewed 50 Asian employers, identified through personal contacts, influential employers sympathetic to the research aims and customers of his family's business. Ram found that the majority had entered into self-employment because 'they felt they had few alternatives'. Although he also found that following the family into business was an important factor in entering into self-employment, Ram claims entering the family business was almost always a last resort and cannot be separated from the unfavourable opportunity structure.

ASIAN SELF-EMPLOYMENT AS AN 'ECONOMIC DEAD-END'

Aldrich et al also sought to explore whether Asians as a group could transform their economic circumstances through self-employment. To appreciate this discussion it is important to bear in mind the political debates of the late 1970s and early 1980s in which the merits of markets and state intervention as a means of improving personal and collective standards of living were discussed. It was a debate, especially in the United States, which was seen to be pertinent to the issue of alleviating racial disadvantage. The Aldrich research team took the view that for the thesis of Asian success as a group through business involvement to be upheld three key criteria would have to be fulfilled (McEvoy et al, 1982:6). Firstly, there would have to be high rates of participation by Asians in retail self-employment. Secondly, most businesses should display signs of economic success. Thirdly, businesses should provide substantial numbers of jobs for other members of the Asian community.

Although they found that the Asian share of retail activity had increased, the increase simply reflected a growth in the local Asian population. Firstly, as the Asian population increased, it was able to support more outlets and also more specialised activities appealing specifically to Asian tastes. Secondly, as it increased, it obtained a larger share of businesses serving the general population. However, they contended that the overall scale of the retail and service sector meant that even where Asians were numerically dominant, these activities never resulted in business ownership for more than a minority of the immigrant community.

Tables 1.1 and 1.2 show the business performance of Asian-owned businesses compared to white-owned businesses.

Table 1.1   Business performance

	White	Asian
Average number of customers per day	152	133
Percentage grossing £750 plus per week	29	41
Percentage making savings from business	50	25
Percentage wishing children to inherit business	26	50
Percentage owning another business	19	22
Percentage in co-operative buying groups	14	14
Average number of employees	2	2
Percentage making profit in previous year	82	72
Percentage expecting profit next year	78	70
Percentage same owner in 1980 as 1978	65	83
Percentage 1978 sites with active business in 1980	90	95

Source: McEvoy et al, 1982:11

Table 1.2   Business inputs

	White	Asian
Average hours worked per week	57	61
Percentage open on Sundays	17	52
Average number of relatives employed	0.61	1.35
Average number working without pay	0.23	0.82
Average days open per week	5.6	6.2
Average hours open per day	8.9	10.1
Average years of education	9.7	10.2
Percentage with degrees	3	20

Source: McEvoy et al, 1982:11

On the basis of the indicators used in Tables 1.1 and 1.2, McEvoy et al (1982:9) concluded that there was no clear distinction between the performances of white and Asian-owned businesses. Moreover, they argued that the tables illustrated clearly that retailing was not only 'small-scale and arduous, but also economically marginal'.

When applying the third criteria for measuring Asian business success, they found that Asian businesses were largely small family-run enterprises which provided few opportunities for employment of non-relative Asians. Hence, McEvoy et al (1982:9) reject the view that Asian involvement in small businesses represents a route into upward mobility and instead argue that it must be seen more as 'a survival mechanism for some Asians, not as a socially propulsive force for the group as a whole'. They argue that because the advantages of property ownership and autonomy are won at a cost of a low income earned only in return for extremely long and unsocial hours of work, 'Asian entrepreneurs are entering not an upward ladder leading to material enrichment, but a dead-end on the fringe of the modern economy' (McEvoy et al, 1982:10). Hence, taking the lead from Marxists, they referred to this social group as the 'lumpen-bourgeoisie', arguing that Asian ethnicity did not provide the basis for overcoming the obstacles and marginalisation that Asians experience:

> ...the socio-economic position of Asians in Britain will not be decided by the resources of the Asian communities themselves: it will be determined by the opportunities afforded by the host society. We accept unconditionally that Asian ethnicity is a source of all manner of positive assets but remain convinced that these will not exert a decisive influence ... business actually represents a waste of capital, talent and energy, by directing them into small shops whose number far exceeds the capacity of the market to support. Asian business is more a confirmation of subordinate status than an escape from it (McEvoy et al, 1982:10).

It will be clear that the concern of these researchers is the success of Asians as a group, and little importance is placed on the possibility that self-employment may provide individuals from ethnic minorities with better employment and economic prospects than they might otherwise have enjoyed.

THE 'CULTURAL RESOURCES' APPROACH:
CHALLENGING THE 'BLOCKED UPWARD MOBILITY' THESIS?

This view of Asian self-employment has, however, been increasingly questioned for offering too one-sided a view of Asian business development and for not acknowledging the very real choices that ethnic minorities may make in deciding to go into business and the line of business they will enter (Werbner, 1990a and 1990b). An alternative approach to understanding Asian entrepreneurship has been put forward which has been referred to as the 'cultural resources' approach. Werbner, in a study of Pakistani entrepreneurship, argues that the critical factors in the success of Pakistani businessmen is their cultural heritage, which stresses thrift, deferred gratification, industriousness and self-reliance (Werbner, 1990a and 1990b). Such attributes no less than the wider environment are seen as central to the development of Asian business.

According to Waldinger et al's interpretation of the 'cultural resources' approach, Asian entrepreneurial activity is seen as likely to develop and succeed if social structures exist through which members of an ethnic group are attached to one another and if these structures can be utilised for economic purposes (Waldinger et al, 1990). They contend that these social structures consist of two parts:

- the networks of kinship and friendship around which communities are arranged and;

- the interlacing of these networks with positions in the economy (jobs), in space (housing) and in civil society (institutions).

The close ties between co-ethnics have three important implications regarding Asian self-employment. Firstly, minorities may be vulnerable and oppressed but they can create resources that offset the harshness of the environment they encounter. Secondly, the social structures of the minority community will spawn organisation. Thirdly, such organisational resources may provide minorities with an added advantage over white kin and community networks (Waldinger et al, 1990:35). The availability of these networks is often made possible through the effects of 'chain migration', whereby the immigration process itself selects immigrants who are integrated into kinship networks through the tendency of immigrants to migrate by means of the sponsorship and assistance of earlier settlers. The use of these kinship and community ties in getting work and other economic opportunities, such as partnership, credit, customers and market information, reinforces the ties of mutual trust, interdependence and reciprocity (Werbner, 1990a).

Some empirical evidence has been emerging to suggest that culture may indeed be key to understanding Asian business development. Srinivasan undertook a survey of small Asian business owners in Oxford in 1989-1990 (Srinivasan, 1992 and 1995). Within the city of Oxford, 83 small shops and 22 restaurants were identified as Asian-owned. This constitutes 12 per cent of shops and restaurants in Oxford while the Asian population makes up 8 per cent of the total population of Oxford. Interviews were carried out with 76 shop and 18 restaurant owners. Detailed information was collected about these self-employed Asians, in terms of their educational and occupational background, their work history, their family and residential patterns, their business practices, their attitudes to racism and assimilation, their ethnic solidarity, their hopes and aspirations.

Srinivasan provides evidence that the success of Asian entrepreneurship cannot simply be measured by economic success and other such 'objective' indicators. Status within the community is an important attribute that is acquired for Asians who enter business and may help to explain why highly educated Asians go into self-employment. Srinivasan found that one in five of her sample were already in professional and managerial jobs when they chose to go into self-employment, in the belief that it gave them added status within their ethnic community. The same motivation was apparent for those who came from working class backgrounds. Furthermore, she found that the independence that small business bestows is particularly important to the ethnic small business owner (Srinivasan, 1992).

The work situation that is described by McEvoy et al (1982) as indicating that Asian businesses operate on the margins of the economy, and therefore have a constant battle for survival, has been interpreted in more positive fashion by Srinivasan. She contends that the whole question of long hours, exploitation of the family and the drudgery of shop-keeping needs to be seen in the light of the benefits that accrue, such as cooperative sharing of work among all family members and the consequent flexibility in hours worked by individual members. Hence, she points to:

> ... the positive aspects of flexible working hours without the necessity of 'clocking in and out', the possibility of dual occupations, a varied social life within the work environment, and for the ethnic shopkeeper, the utilisation of female labour within cultural constraints, and a position of power vis-à-vis the white customers (Srinivasan, 1992:68).

However, the 'cultural resources' approach has come under criticism. Such theories, it is claimed, underestimate the impact that racial discrimination in all its forms may have on the development of ethnic groupings and the reliance on 'community' resources for survival. If opportunities for mainstream employment are not open to ethnic minorities because of racism, 'then the adaptation of available skills and resources within a particular group to alternative income generating mechanisms is a reasonably predictable outcome' (Phizacklea, 1990:85). Hence, Jones and McEvoy (1991) conclude that ethnic enterprise almost invariably arises out of a context of disadvantage as a means of circumventing barriers in the wider job market. Ethnic entrepreneurs often find themselves boxed in, their choices constrained by the racism of white dominated society. In order to survive, many immigrants have been prepared to take over the jobs and premises left by white workers and employers, and tolerate low wages and poor conditions. According to Ram, 'rather than having a cultural flair for enterprise, it seems that minority groups have been sucked into sectors like clothing and retailing through the limitation of real choices' (Ram, 1992:603).

ASIAN BUSINESSES: SUCCESS OR FAILURE?

The 'economic dead end' thesis which represents Asian businesses as firms struggling to survive on the fringes of the modern economy has also been criticised by reference to large-scale survey findings. It has been argued that, whatever may be the reasons for entry into self-employment and whatever may be the nature of the opportunity and resource structures available to Asians, judged by outcomes some Asian self-employment has been an economic success (Modood, 1991). Data from the Labour Force Survey, the Census and the Fourth National Survey of Ethnic Minorities suggest, for example, that African Asians and Indians were almost one and a half times more likely than whites to be self-employed and to have employees (Jones, 1993:95, table 4.6; Owen, 1993:5; Modood et al, 1997).

However, this success in business has not been uniform across all the different Asian groups (Modood, 1991). Although the last decade has witnessed a substantial growth in Asian self-employment, it is not evenly spread across all Asian groups. Pakistanis have the same, and Bangladeshis a lower rate of self-employment nationally than whites (Jones, 1993; Owen, 1993; Modood et al, 1997). Moreover, the Fourth Survey has found that in its sample of 200 white and over 300 Asian self-employed, the mean weekly earnings of Pakistanis were substantially lower than those of whites; for African Asians they were higher; and for Indians substantially higher than for whites. Critically, each of the Indians had higher mean earnings in self-employment than in paid employment, Pakistanis about the same, and while the opposite was the case for African Asians, white self-employed had the greater negative earnings differential compared to employees of their own group (Modood et al, 1997). The Asian groups may indeed have increased their share in the small-scale retail sector: the confectioner, Mars, estimated that by the end of the 1980s Asians owned 65 per cent of the independent retail outlets in the country, including 95 per cent of outlets in London. They have, however, also diversified into other sectors, so that by 1994, only half of Asian self-employment was in retail.

Also relevant here is a study undertaken in Leicestershire, an area with a substantial East African Asian population, which found that Asian firms have grown significantly faster than white firms of a similar size in the same industries (Ward, 1987).

ACCOUNTING FOR DIFFERENCES AMONG
DIFFERENT ASIAN GROUPS

In a study of self-employment in Bradford Rafiq found an under-representation of Muslims (Rafiq, 1992). In comparison with their share of 77 per cent of the Asian population in Bradford, he found that only 64 per cent of the 1,100 Asian businesses belonged to Muslims, the remainder being owned by Sikhs and Hindus. Moreover, when the 1,100 Asian businesses were broken down into small (that is small retail and services outlets) and large (that is manufacturers, wholesalers, large retailers and limited liability companies) businesses, it was found that Indians and East Africans (that is non-Muslim Asians) were not only over-represented in entrepreneurial activity, but tended to be concentrated in larger businesses, whereas Pakistanis and Bangladeshis (Muslim Asians) had on average smaller businesses.

Rafiq, however, rejected motivational factors as being important in explaining these differences, not because he considered cultural factors irrelevant to motivation, but because he claimed all Asian groups receive strong cultural support to enter business. Instead, he suggested that these differences in participation rates can only be explained through the difference in the socio-economic status of Muslim and non-Muslim Asians. Rafiq defines socio-economic status as encompassing economic resources and class attributes such as levels of education. According to this argument, the greater the resources of a minority group, the more likely they are to enter business. Hence, it is because non-Muslim Asians have a higher socio-economic position than Muslim Asians that explains why there are differential rates of entry into self-employment.

Related factors, important in understanding Asian entrepreneurship, were found by Basu (1995) in her survey of 78 small businesses in 1994. These businesses were in the retail, distribution and catering sectors, located in and around London. She relied on personal contacts and a snowballing technique to identify respondents and the interviews were carried out using a detailed questionnaire. Sixty-seven per cent of respondents were

Indian, 18 per cent Pakistani and 12 per cent Bangladeshi. She found that:

> ... entrepreneurial entry into small-scale businesses in the retail and catering sectors was influenced by previous employment experience in that line of business; the entrant's perception of the relatively low barriers to entering and operating this sort of business and the advice received from informal sources such as family or community members and friends who were already in business ... The significant reliance on internal sources of finance in starting such relatively small business ventures and the respondents' experience with bankers at the time of business entry suggests that the initial choice regarding business size was constrained by the access to formal sources of finance (Basu, 1995:20).

She also found that the greater the personal risk taken by the entrepreneur in terms of investing their own personal money in the business venture, the more likely he or she is to be motivated to make a success of the venture and, hence, the higher the chances of achieving success. However, there was a weak link between funding from informal sources like family and business success, leading Basu to argue:

> ... entrepreneurs are basically self-seeking profit maximisers who are interested in maximising the return on their own investment. Consequently, as soon as their own risk or investment is diluted, their incentive to maximise returns weakens and hence, the less likely they are to achieve business success (Basu, 1995:22).

Basu also found a strong positive relationship between the level of educational qualifications of the entrepreneur and success, lending support to Rafiq's hypothesis. She noted that this was an interesting finding given the relatively low technical skill requirements of small retail distribution businesses. Furthermore, there was a positive link between business success and the proportion of family members in the same line of business, suggesting support for arguments emphasising family, community and culture.

ASIAN SELF-EMPLOYMENT: THE INTERACTION OF CULTURE AND ECONOMICS

An important development that emerges from the preceding discussion is that a relatively more interactive approach is required to the effects of culture and external constraints, such as the local opportunity structure and discrimination in the wider labour market, if we are fully to understand Asian business development.

Waldinger et al (1990:21) have suggested an approach which combines the economic and ethnicity perspectives. Their interactive approach to understanding minority business development is built on two dimensions: opportunity structures and characteristics of the ethnic group. Opportunity structures consist of market conditions that may favour products or services oriented towards 'co-ethnics' and situations in which a wider, non-ethnic market might be served. Opportunity structures also include the routes through which access to business is obtained. Group characteristics include pre-migration circumstances, a group's reaction to conditions in the host society, and resource mobilisation through various features of the ethnic community. They contend that ethnic strategies emerge from the interaction of all these factors, as ethnic entrepreneurs adapt to the resources made available in opportunity structures and attempt to carve out their own niches.

Against this background, the Policy Studies Institute conducted a study to help explain the diversity between Asian groups in Britain in the extent of self-employment and in the size of businesses. The Fourth National Survey of Ethnic Minorities was conducted by PSI and SCPR in 1994. The Fourth Survey was a representative national survey of ethnic minorities which, along with other aspects of economic activity, covered self-employment. It included over 300 self-employed South Asians among its respondents. The current study is based on revisiting a sample of these respondents for a second interview in the summer of 1995. Altogether 129 new interviews were achieved. Two-fifths of these were in London and a fifth in the West Midlands. The remainder of the interviews were in Manchester, Stoke, Bradford, Leeds, Leicester and Harborough in Leicestershire, and Gravesham and Gillingham in Kent. Fifty-three of the interviewees were Indian,

36 were African Asian, 33 were Pakistani and 7 were Bangladeshi. Owing to the size of the Bangladeshi sample, differences between Bangladeshis and other South Asian groups could not be examined. However, Bangladeshis are included in all figures referring to South Asians in our analyses. We would like to stress that this data should not be used to draw any conclusions about Bangladeshi self-employed in Britain.

Further details about the design of the sample and other aspects of the research method can be found in the Appendix at the end of the book.

RESEARCH AIMS

With a comparative focus on the similarities and differences between Pakistanis, Indians and African Asians we wished, firstly, to understand better the relative influence of cultural and economic factors on self-employment. This involved examining the extent to which self-employment is a positive choice, seen as offering benefits (economic, psychological and social), and the extent to which it is a result of labour market difficulties and racial discrimination; how economic, social and religious factors affect the nature of self-employment and outcomes; and how familial roles encourage and facilitate self-employment.

Secondly, we wished to examine the extent to which self-employment is a vehicle for employment not only for the self-employed themselves, but also for others as employees and family workers.

Thirdly, we wish to explore the extent to which self-employment provides upward mobility, where upward mobility is defined in terms of the respondents' aspirations as well as in terms of income, occupational status and social status.

The objective of the research is to contribute to discussions about inequalities in Britain and the extent to which upward socio-economic mobility is possible, especially for groups who suffer racial discrimination. We hope thereby to improve the basis for developing employment policies aimed at lessening racial disadvantage and promoting opportunities for ethnic minorities.

Chapter 2

CHARACTERISTICS OF THE SOUTH ASIAN SELF-EMPLOYED SAMPLE

The Fourth National Survey of Ethnic Minorities (1994) found that self-employment among South Asians, which had taken off in the late 1970s, had continued to grow, especially among Pakistanis. A third of the Pakistani, Indian, and African Asian men in paid work were self-employed. While the same was true for Chinese men, it contrasted with a fifth of the white and Bangladeshi, and an eighth of the Caribbean men in paid work who were self-employed (Modood et al, 1997). Most groups of women were less than half as likely as their male counterparts to be self-employed, but in their case too there was a similar ethnic pattern. While some of the recent growth in self-employment consists of 'contracted-out' workers, workers who are nominally self-employed but who in practice work for a single employer, this in fact applied more to whites than to Asians (see Table 2.1). Among the nominally self-employed, South Asian men and women were more likely than whites to be sole traders and employers. A related finding of the Fourth Survey was that South Asians were almost twice as likely as whites to be conducting self-employment from separate business premises.

This study is based on interviews with 129 self-employed South Asians. Most of these interviews were re-interviews with respondents of the Fourth Survey, the remainder being partners and associates of the original respondents. The profile of the respondents to the survey should not be seen as representative of the South Asian self-employed in Britain. However, the way in which the sample was drawn would lead the sample to provide a reasonable picture of the characteristics of self-employed Asians across the areas of the country where their concentration is highest. The Fourth Survey found, however, that the rates of Asian self-employment were highest in areas of low ethnic minority residence. These businesses were also larger and created more jobs, with half having employees as opposed to only a third among those in above average minority density areas (Modood et al, 1997). Most Asians, however, live in areas of above average minority density, and our sample is drawn from seven such areas in England. The study offers, therefore, a picture that is true of the majority of Asian self-employed, but does not claim to be nationally representative.

Table 2.1   Type of self-employment

		column percentages
	White	South Asian
Men		
Contractee	37	20
Sole trader	37	42
Employer	26	37
Weighted count	166	271
Unweighted count	144	267
Women		
Contractee	21	13
Sole trader	51	54
Employer	28	34
Weighted count	62	63
Unweighted count	60	55

This chapter presents the characteristics of those respondents: age, ethnicity, religion and gender, their background and migration to the UK. Details about family size and the children of respondents are also given.

PERSONAL CHARACTERISTICS OF THE SAMPLE

Table 2.2 shows the ethnic origin of the sample: 41 per cent described themselves as Indian; 28 per cent as African Asian; 26 per cent as Pakistani and 5 per cent as Bangladeshi. This distribution broadly reflects that of self-employed South Asians nationally (Modood et al, 1997). A consequence was that there were too few Bangladeshis in our sample for any separate analysis, and while they are included in the findings relating to South Asians as a whole, this study is unable to offer any inter-group comparisons regarding Bangladeshi self-employment.

Table 2.2   The distribution of the self-employed sample, by ethnic group

	Indian	African Asian	Pakistani	Bangladeshi
Percentage	41	28	26	5
Unweighted base	*53*	*36*	*33*	*7*

Most of the self-employed were male (84 per cent) (Table 2.3). However, there were more female owners among Indians (25 per cent) than there were among African Asians (14 per cent) and Pakistanis (9 per cent). Again, this reflected the national picture, as found by the Fourth Survey (Modood et al, 1997).

Table 2.3   Gender of the self-employed, by ethnic group

				column percentages
	Indian	African Asian	Pakistani	All South Asians
Male	75	86	91	84
Female	25	14	9	16
Unweighted base	*53*	*36*	*33*	*129*

Table 2.4 shows that almost half the sample of self-employed were aged between 35 and 44 and a total of four-fifths were over the age of 35. There was little variation in the age profile of the self-employed across ethnic groups, apart from the Pakistanis having a slightly younger age profile than Indians or African Asians.

Table 2.4   Age of the self-employed, by ethnic group

column percentages

	Indian	African Asian	Pakistani	All South Asians
Under 25	4	3	3	3
25 - 34	15	19	24	19
35 - 44	50	47	39	46
45 - 54	21	19	21	19
55 +	10	11	12	12
Unweighted base	*48*	*36*	*33*	*124*

Aldrich et al in 1978 found that one of the major explanations of Asian entry into self-employment was the desire to avoid racial discrimination and the resulting confinement to low status jobs in the labour market (Aldrich et al, 1981:175). The key factor used by Aldrich et al in this explanation was the existence of a relatively large number of well-qualified South Asian shopkeepers compared to the more poorly-educated white shopkeepers in their sample. Specifically, Aldrich et al (1981:177) found that 20 per cent of South Asian business owners in their sample were graduates compared to only 3 per cent of their white sample. Later research has shown there is a strong correlation between educational qualifications and success in self-employment among Asians (Rafiq, 1992; Basu, 1995).

Table 2.5 shows that a significant majority of South Asian business owners were well qualified with nearly two-thirds having formal qualifications of some sort. This comprised nearly a fifth who were graduates; a further fifth with 'A' levels and a quarter with 'O' levels. Some degree of variation emerged across the different ethnic groups when higher qualifications were con-

Table 2.5   The education levels of the South Asian self-employed

column percentages

	Indian	African Asian	Pakistani	All South Asians
Degree	15	28	15	18
A level or equiv. or higher ed. below degree	25	17	9	18
O-level or equiv.	32	11	24	24
None or below O-level	28	44	51	40
Unweighted base	*53*	*36*	*33*	*129*

sidered, with twice as many African Asians (28 per cent) reporting being graduates as Indians and Pakistanis (15 per cent).
Interestingly, a degree of bi-polarisation was evident among the
African Asian sample with over two-fifths (44 per cent) of them
also reporting they had no qualifications. Compared to the
migrants from the same ethnic groups in the Fourth Survey, the
Indian and Pakistani self-employed were more likely to have
qualifications than their peers, but the African Asians were no
more likely. On the other hand, while the Indian self-employed
were less likely to have a degree than other Indian migrants, the
African Asian self-employed sample, and especially the Pakistanis,
were much more likely (Modood et al, 1997).

IMMIGRATION

Almost all our sample were born abroad (97 per cent). Of the
Indians, 92 per cent were born in India, 6 per cent in Britain and
2 per cent in another non-European country. The country of
birth of African Asians was more diverse with two-thirds being
born in Africa and the remaining third in the Indian subcontinent. In the case of Pakistanis, nearly all reported their country of
birth as being Pakistan.

Although migration from the Indian subcontinent began in the
late 1950s, the majority of South Asians came to Britain in the
1960s and 1970s (Jones, 1993:25). As Table 2.6 shows, three-

quarters of the self-employed migrated to Britain between 1965 and 1979, with little variation across the different minority groups. About one in six of the self-employed, mainly Indians and Pakistanis, migrated before 1965, while about one in twelve came to Britain after 1979. On average, African Asians had migrated slightly more recently than Indians and Pakistanis.

Table 2.6   The year of entry into the UK of the self-employed, by ethnic group

				column percentages
	Indian	African Asian	Pakistani	All South Asians
Before 1965	19	3	28	16
1965-1979	73	86	69	76
1980 to present	8	11	3	8
Unweighted base	*48*	*36*	*32*	*123*

Most of the, now, self-employed were children or young adults when they came to Britain. Many came to reunite with their families, in particular to reunite with their fathers and grandfathers who had invariably arrived earlier, thus confirming the view of anthropological researchers that the South Asian migration to Britain was a 'chain migration' through kinship networks (Watson, 1977). About one in seven (14 per cent) said they came to Britain for education, while less than one fifth (18 per cent) said the reason for coming to Britain was employment opportunities (Table 2.7).

There was some difference between ethnic groups in the reasons for coming to Britain: about twice as many Pakistanis (28 per cent) as Indians (12 per cent) and African Asians (14 per cent) mentioned job opportunities, while education (25 per cent) and political circumstances (19 per cent) were more likely to be mentioned by African Asians than other groups. The relatively high proportion of African Asians who cited political circumstances as a major factor in coming to Britain was as a consequence of their expulsion from Kenya in the late 1960s and Uganda in the early 1970s (Bhachu, 1986). Family reasons for coming to the UK were more likely to be mentioned by Indians (68 per cent) than African Asians (47 per cent) and Pakistanis (53 per cent).

Table 2.7   The reasons for migrating to Britain, by ethnic group

column percentages

	Indian	African Asian	Pakistani	All South Asians
Family reasons	68	47	53	58
Job opportunities	12	14	28	18
For education	10	25	1	14
Political factors	8	19	0	9
Other	10	14	16	12
Unweighted base	*50*	*36*	*32*	*125*

Respondents were allowed to specify more than one reason, therefore the column totals need not equal 100 per cent.

Given the age of the self-employed when they migrated to Britain, it was not surprising that the majority were in full-time education immediately prior to emigration (69 per cent) (Table 2.8). Of the remainder, most were working and very few were unemployed. There was some variation across ethnic groups with more Indians coming from employment (24 per cent) than African Asians (14 per cent) or Pakistanis (9 per cent). Conversely, more Pakistanis (78 per cent) and African Asians (72 per cent) than Indians (62 per cent) came from full-time education when they migrated to Britain. Only 6 per cent of the sample were self-employed in their previous country on emigrating to Britain, which is a third of all those that were in work, though given the small proportion that were economically active before migration, it is difficult to deduce a propensity to self-employment from just this fact.

Table 2.8   Economic activity prior to migration to Britain, by ethnic group

	Indian	African Asian	Pakistani	All South Asians
				column percentages
Full-time education	62	72	78	69
Working	24	14	9	18
Unemployed	0	3	0	1
Looking after the home	6	6	0	4
Something else	8	6	13	8
Unweighted base	*50*	*36*	*32*	*125*

ECONOMIC ACTIVITY PRIOR TO SELF-EMPLOYMENT

Previous employment history is likely to be an important influence on self-employment: affecting whether an individual is interested in establishing their own business; providing skills and knowledge which affect the nature of the business established and its success. Factors relating to specific skills are discussed in subsequent chapters. Here we look at general employment and supervisory experience. Respondents were asked about their employment history, going back three years prior to them setting up in business.

Seven out of ten of the self-employed had worked as an employee for some or all of the time in the three years prior to setting up in business (as their main job) (Table 2.9). This did not vary by ethnic group. For most of these, employment had been fairly stable and nine in ten reported they had had just one job, while the remainder reported they had had between two and four jobs. Part-time working was rare, with only 2 per cent having worked part-time at any time over this period.

Table 2.9   Economic activity in the three years prior to self-
             employment

column percentages

	Indian	African Asian	Pakistani	All South Asians
Employee	69	69	75	71
Unemployed	14	19	19	16
Full-time education	14	19	9	14
None of these	21	11	6	13
Unweighted base	*52*	*36*	*32*	*126*

Columns need not sum to 100, as over three years individuals may have had more than one economic activity status.

The high proportion lacking experience as an employee was partly due to the number in full-time education: 14 per cent had been in full-time education at least some of the time during the three years preceding entry into self-employment. Most of these (59 per cent) had been in full-time education for two to three years of this period. Moreover, 8 per cent of the whole sample entered self-employment directly from full-time education.

However, about one in six of the sample (16 per cent) experienced at least one period of unemployment during the three years prior to entering self-employment as a main job, and 9 per cent entered self-employment directly from unemployment. Half (11 out of 20) of those that had been unemployed said it had been for a duration of more than six months, although most reported not having been unemployed on more than one or two occasions during this period. This concurs with analyses of other data sources. The Labour Force Survey has shown over several years that the movement into self-employment is not usually from unemployment, with the unemployed averaging about one sixth of the flow into self-employment in the 1980s (Hakim, 1989:287; Meager et al, 1994; Campbell and Daly, 1992). Robinson's combined analysis of Census and Labour Force Survey data led him to conclude that 'contrary to the thesis that ethnics take to self-employment because of failure in the waged-labour sector, fewer Asians and West Indians [than whites] move from unemployment to self-employment' (Robinson, 1990:283), which seems to be consistent with our sample. Finally, 14 per cent said they were neither working nor in full-time education but doing something else, for example looking after the home.

Management and supervisory experience can be a very important influence on the success of the business. Most South Asian business owners had little experience of managing or supervising the work of others prior to entering into business: more than seven out of eight had not supervised anyone in their three years prior to self-employment (Table 2.10).

Table 2.10   The proportion of self-employed who were supervisors in the three years prior to self-employment

			column percentages	
	Indian	African Asian	Pakistani	All South Asians
Number supervised				
0	90	86	84	87
1 - 5	2	3	0	3
6 - 10	4	9	3	5
11 or more	2	3	13	5
Unweighted base	*51*	*35*	*32*	*126*

THE SELF-EMPLOYED AND THEIR CHILDREN

Children may play an important role in South Asian self-employment: providing motivation to become self-employed and to develop the business (either for financial reasons or in order to provide family employment) and providing the means to supply the business with labour. These issues are investigated in later chapters. This section describes the children of the self-employed, concentrating on aspects pertinent to the family business.

Almost all the sample of South Asian self-employed reported having children (92 per cent), with no difference across ethnic groups (Table 2.11). However, Pakistanis tended to have larger families: most Indians and African Asian families consisted of one or two children and more than three was rare, whereas most Pakistani families contained four or five children. This contrast is, in fact, a characteristic of these groups rather than just of the self-employed among them (Modood et al, 1997).

Table 2.11 Family size, by ethnic group

				column percentages
	Indian	African Asian	Pakistani	All South Asians
Number of children				
none	6	8	9	9
1-2	47	50	12	37
3	26	33	15	24
4-5	17	6	48	24
6 or more	4	3	15	6
Unweighted base	*53*	*36*	*33*	*129*

The age of children may influence self-employment, with self-employment providing flexibility over the care of younger children, and older children providing a source of assistance. Seventy per cent of the self-employed had children aged 11 or over, with most having up to three in this age group (Table 2.12). African Asians were less likely to have children as a potential source of assistance in the business: only 60 per cent had children aged 11 or over compared with 75 per cent of Indians and 73 per cent of Pakistanis. Pakistanis tended to have more children in this age group, with African Asians having the least.

In total, 89 self-employed South Asians had 223 children aged 11 and over between them. Of these children, over half were aged between 11 and 18 (58 per cent), over one third aged 19 to 29 (37 per cent) and only 4 per cent were aged 30 or more. There was no significant difference by ethnic group in the age profile. Over half the children were male (54 per cent), with Pakistanis having a particularly high proportion of male children in this age group (59 per cent).

Table 2.12   The number of children aged 11 or over, by ethnic group

column percentages

	Indian	African Asian	Pakistani	All South Asians
Number of children aged 11 or over				
none	25	40	27	30
1-2	46	40	27	40
3	17	20	12	16
4+	13	0	30	13
Unweighted base	*53*	*35*	*33*	*128*

The children of the self-employed were particularly likely to participate in post-compulsory full-time education (Table 2.13). The overwhelming majority of 16-22 year olds were in full-time education, with relatively few in paid work or unemployed. The numbers in the sample are too small for percentage analysis by ethnic groups, but as can be seen from Table 2.13, the children of the Pakistani self-employed were less likely than the others to be in full-time education, and more likely to be unemployed. This is consistent with national data on staying-on rates and rates of unemployment among South Asian groups (Modood et al, 1997). The higher rate of unemployment among the Pakistanis was also found among the off-spring of the self-employed who were 23 years old or over: 7 out of 12 Pakistanis compared to 3 out of 35 Indians/African Asians were unemployed.

Table 2.13   Employment status of children between 16-22 years old, by ethnic group

absolute numbers

	Indian	African Asian	Pakistani	All South Asians
In full-time education	32	11	15	58
In paid work	3	3	4	10
Unemployed	-	-	6	6
Unweighted base	*35*	*14*	*25*	*74*

The higher level of unemployment among the Pakistanis did not seem to be related to their level of qualifications. The Pakistanis were more likely to have a degree or similar qualification, and not much more likely than Indians to have a qualification below A level or equivalent – though again the sizes are relatively small and include those who are still studying for further qualifications (Table 2.14). Taking the sample as a whole, it does seem that the children of the self-employed are particularly well qualified. In this respect they are like their parents – with perhaps the important difference that the children's qualifications are likely to be British, while in the case of most of their parents they are likely to have been from overseas (Modood et al, 1997).

Table 2.14 **The highest qualification of children aged 18 or over, by ethnic group**

				column percentages
	Indian	African Asian	Pakistani	All South Asians
Higher education qualification	14	14	22	17
A level or equiv	39	50	22	34
O level or equiv	11	14	27	18
Below O level or none	36	21	30	32
Unweighted base	*44*	*14*	*37*	*95*

SUMMARY

The sample of self-employed reflected the national composition of Asian self-employment in terms of ethnic and gender composition. However, it should not be seen as a representative sample, as it was confined to areas of high concentrations of Asian self-employment.

The self-employed sample consisted mainly of prime age married males with children. Nearly all were migrants to Britain, mainly emigrating when a child or young adult and arriving in Britain before 1980. For the majority, the reasons for coming to

Britain were primarily familial, to reunite with their fathers and grandfathers who had emigrated earlier. Most were still in full-time education when they emigrated. However, a minority came to Britain for economic reasons, for job opportunities, although very few had been unemployed prior to emigrating. This picture was similar across ethnic groups except for two factors. Firstly, women made up a higher proportion of the self-employed among Indians than Pakistanis or African Asians and, secondly, economic reasons for migrating featured more often for Pakistanis, and political reasons for African Asians.

In terms of the skills (through qualifications) brought to self-employment, the sample was more diverse. Although over one third had no qualifications, as many as one sixth had degrees (or similar). Pakistanis were the least qualified group, while African Asians showed a bipolar pattern, with a high proportion holding degrees (or similar) as well as a high proportion being unqualified. Employment experience was less varied. A remarkably high proportion had not been an employee during the three years prior to self-employment (29 per cent), with 14 per cent having been in full-time education for some or all of the three years, and 16 per cent had experienced unemployment in this time. Few had had the experience of supervising others.

Typically, the self-employed were married men with one to three children. However, there was a marked difference between Pakistanis on the one hand and Indians and African Asians on the other, with the former tending to have a larger number of children. Seventy per cent had children aged 11 and over, of whom the majority were aged under 19. Pakistani families tended to have more children aged at least 11 than did other ethnic groups. The children had a high level of full-time participation in post-16 education and were well qualified. However, a higher proportion of Pakistani children were unemployed and this did not appear to be related to their age or qualifications achieved.

Chapter 3

CULTURE AND ATTITUDES OF THE SELF-EMPLOYED

While some have explained entry into self-employment as the lack of satisfactory alternatives driving South Asians into self-employment, with racism playing a part (Aldrich et al, 1981; Ram, 1992; Jones et al, 1994), others have identified cultural factors as playing a major role. The cultural factors that ethnic relations research has tended to focus on are, however, very different to the sociological debate about political individualism and whether there exists an 'enterprise culture' (see, for example, Bechhofer et al, 1974; Scase and Goffee, 1981; Blanchflower and Oswald, 1990; Burrows (ed), 1991). Waldinger et al (1991) have identified networks of friendship and kinship as both predisposing people towards and assisting self-employment. The importance of the family in particular has emerged from a number of studies. A study of a number of migrant ethnic groups in the US has suggested that 'the family is an institution that embodies an important form of social capital that immigrants draw on in the pursuit of economic advancement' (Sanders and Nee, 1996:233). This would mean identifying not just the cultural importance of family to South Asians of the kind that we found in an earlier study (Modood, Beishon and Virdee, 1994), but also some comparison between a commitment to the family and other things important in one's life. Specifically, one would need to explore the connections between pro-family attitudes and the economic value of the family. For example, Afshar has argued in connection with Pakistani women, including the young, professionals and, even, feminists, that there is an overwhelming acceptance 'as "natural" that they should contribute their labour and their income to the family and that the family had a right to extract such surplus from daughters and mothers alike' (Afshar, 1989:222). Other factors too, such as trust and status, have been identified as features of South Asian cultures which may also pre-dispose entry into business and ultimately help to explain its success (Werbner, 1990a and 1990b; Srinivasan, 1992).

Taking these approaches as a starting point, this chapter describes the cultural and familial background of the South Asian self-employed. Some of the key components of culture discussed include strength of religious belief and how it may influence the business; the degree to which a business was a vehicle for the strengthening of family cohesion and solidarity; the attitudes of business owners to their daughters and wife working in the business compared to in the external labour market; the extent to which South Asians trust members of their own community compared to non-members, and finally, the South Asian entrepreneur's general outlook on life and how it may shape an economic perspective, not least the perception of risk. While the relevance of these factors to self-employment is discussed, the linkage between culture and self-employment for our sample is made in the subsequent chapters on start-up, business development and success.

RELIGION

Religion may affect business in many ways, affecting owners' general outlook on life and, depending on the religion, prescribing and proscribing certain activities. Research has clearly established that religion represents a major component in the formation of an ethnic identity, particularly among the migrant South Asian population (Modood, Beishon and Virdee, 1994). This study confirms the importance of religion to the self-employed: almost nine-tenths of the sample said they had a religion and almost four out of five said that religion was important to them (Tables 3.1 and 3.2).

Table 3.1   **The religion of the self-employed, by ethnic group**

column percentages

	Indian	African	Pakistani Asian	All South Asians
No religion	26	3	0	12
Muslim	4	17	100	36
Hindu	32	44	0	26
Sikh	38	28	0	23
Christian	0	3	0	1
Jain	0	6	0	2
Unweighted base	*53*	*36*	*33*	*129*

Table 3.2   **Percentage of self-employed who said religion was important**

column percentages

	Indian	African Asian	Pakistani	All South Asians
Not important	32	22	6	22
Fairly important	45	50	0	34
Very important	23	28	94	44
Unweighted base	*53*	*36*	*33*	*129*

There were significant religious differences across ethnic groups. Firstly, Indians were less likely to identify with any religion: over one quarter of Indians did not have a religion, compared with almost all African Asians and Pakistanis who had a religion. Secondly, the religion and range of religions ascribed to by each group varied. All Pakistanis were Muslim and nearly all Indians were Sikh or Hindu. The religious affiliation of the African Asians was more diverse: while over two-thirds were Hindu or Sikh, a large minority were Muslim, Christian or Jain. Lastly, the degree of importance attributed to religion varied: while nearly all Pakistanis reported that religion was very important to them, most Indians and African Asians who were religious saw it as fairly (rather than very) important. Indeed, among those subscribing to a religion, African Asians seemed least likely to see religion as important, making them overall much closer to Indians than Pakistanis on the importance of religion.[1]

Table 3.3   Religion and business issues

	Indian	African Asian	Pakistani	All
				percentage of each ethnic group
Religion has a view on handling alcohol	8	32	97	41
Religion has a view on handling meat/meat products	16	41	87	44
Religion has a view on lending or borrowing money for interest	2	15	75	28
*Unweighted base**	*51*	*34*	*32*	*123*

* Base varied slightly over questions: base is those self-employed at the time of the survey.

People's beliefs about their own religion were explored in relation to certain activities relevant to business activities, namely, the handling of alcohol, the handling of certain meats and meat products; and to usury (the lending or borrowing of money for (excessive) interest). At least two out of five of the self-employed said that their religion had a view on the handling of alcohol and on the handling of meat or meat products (Table 3.3). The handling of alcohol as a religious issue was largely confined to Muslims and almost all Muslims identified it as an issue. The handling of certain meats and meat products was also an issue for a large majority of Muslims, although this affected other religions to a greater extent than did alcohol. Usury as a religious issue was confined to Muslims, although this was an issue for a smaller majority than either alcohol or meat. More than three-quarters of Muslims said that their religion has a view on the lending or borrowing of money for interest. This reflects the fact that the Qur'an bans certain exploitive forms of lending, and possibly all forms of lending where interest is earned without the lender sharing any of the risk faced by the borrower (Kuran, 1995:157). In recent years, in fact, an Islamic conception of banking has been developed based on the principle that it is unjust to earn money without assuming risk. Islamic economists, therefore, favour venture capitalism (where the lender takes equity in the borrower's business) but consider it 'unjust for a bank to earn interest on an industrial loan, for the arrangement places the risk of the financed venture entirely on the industrialist, allowing the bank to earn a return even if the venture fails' (Kuran, 1995:157). The underlying principle is: no risk, no profit.

However, the fact that religion was considered to have a view on an issue did not necessarily mean that this would influence business activity, either because the religious view was not put into practice or because the issue did not arise. The extent to which religion did affect business, in respect of the above issues and in other ways, is discussed in the next chapter.

FAMILY HISTORY OF SELF-EMPLOYMENT

A family history of self-employment gives individuals familiarity with the demands of self-employment. It may also enable individuals to develop skills important to business development and provide access to advice, as well as encouragement. Indeed, family involvement in self-employment has been shown to be a strong indicator of whether other members of the family go on to enter self-employment (Basu, 1995).

A high proportion of the self-employed came from families where others had already been self-employed (Table 3.4). Just over half of the South Asian business owners in this sample said they had had at least one family relative engaged in self-employment: a higher proportion of Pakistanis (63 per cent) and African Asians (58 per cent) reported family involvement in business than Indians (48 per cent).

While a family history of self-employment might encourage and assist self-employment, the quality of the family and business connections are also important. The study explored further businesses of relatives in which the self-employed respondent had either worked or which were in a similar line to their own business.

Table 3.4   Proportion with relatives that have been self-employed

				column percentages
	Indian	African Asian	Pakistani	All South Asians
Had self-employed relative	48	58	63	53
Previously worked in family business	19	23	9	16
Weighted base	*48*	*31*	*32*	*118*

About one in six (16 per cent) reported having some experience of actually working in these family-run businesses, with a greater proportion of Indians (19 per cent) and African Asians (23 per cent) stating this than Pakistanis (9 per cent). These 19 people had worked in a total of 25 family-owned businesses between them. Forty per cent of these businesses (9 out of 25) were run by the respondent's parents and half (13) were in an area of business that the respondents subsequently chose for themselves. However, experience was not always extensive: just over half said they had worked in the family business for less than one year; a further third between one and four years; only one in six had more than five years' involvement.

A further 14 per cent (16 out of 118) had relatives who had run a business which was in a similar line to their own, although they themselves had never worked in those businesses. About one third of these businesses (10 out of the 32 for which details were given) were owned by the respondent's mother or father.

It seems, then, that few of our sample had extensive past experience in working or helping to run a business owned by a family member. However about one fifth may have benefited from access to knowledge specific to the business they themselves would eventually own, through having relatives in the same line of business, and that the high proportion with relatives in business at all encouraged or assisted self-employment.

SELF AND FAMILY

Entrepreneurs are often typified as individualistic, money-motivated people. Self-employment can make different demands on the individual compared with working as an employee: time commitment, planning, stress. At the same time it may offer different benefits: greater control, employment for the family, income, for example. Attitudes to the family, social life and income may affect self-employment. For example, commitment to the family and general familial solidarity are important aspects of South Asian cultures (Modood, Beishon and Virdee, 1994). In particular, it has been argued that one of the major reasons that explain why South Asians are over-represented in retail self-employment is because of the degree to which family life is strengthened by working together (Srinivasan, 1992). In this section, general attitudes to life are described. These are linked to business development and success in Chapters 5 and 6.

Both work and family were very important to a high proportion (around 90 per cent) of the self-employed (Table 3.5). Money, leisure and friends were considered very important by up to a half only. However, with one exception, these factors were considered as at least quite important by 95 per cent of respondents. The one exception was leisure, which 16 per cent considered to be not very important to their lives.

Table 3.5 The importance of work, family, friends, leisure and money
column percentages

	Indian	African Asian	Pakistani	All South Asians
Factor seen as very important				
Family	87	97	91	91
Work	83	92	85	87
Money	46	50	49	50
Leisure	59	42	23	42
Friends	45	42	31	39
*Unweighted base**	*53*	*36*	*33*	*129*

* Base varied: down to 51 for Indians, 33 for African Asians, 31 for Pakistanis and 6 for Bangladeshis (minimum 123 for total).

Respondents were asked to classify each item as very important, quite important or not very important in their life.

While work and family assumed great importance to most people in each ethnic group, looking at all these factors together, leisure and friends seem to assume more importance in the lives of Indians than other groups. Indeed, a relatively high proportion of African Asians and Pakistanis saw leisure as not very important in their lives (14 per cent and 23 per cent respectively, compared with 8 per cent of Indians) and significantly more Indians placed leisure as very important rather than money.

Table 3.6   Duty to self versus duty to family

Respondents were asked which of the following two statements they most agreed with. Statement A: *"Everyone has a duty to do what is best for their family even at the expense of their own well-being."* Statement B: *"Everyone has a life of their own and should not be asked to sacrifice their own well-being for the sake of their family."*

	Indian	African Asian	Pakistani	*column percentages* All South Asians
Agreed most with Statement A	65	69	74	67
Agreed equally with both	19	19	3	17
Agreed most with Statement B	15	11	23	17
Unweighted base	*52*	*36*	*31*	*126*

While family was very important to such a high proportion, individualism was more important to about one in six. Table 3.6 shows that two-thirds of all South Asians (67 per cent) support the view that everyone has a duty to do what is best for their family even at the expense of their own well-being, compared to about one sixth (17 per cent) who reported that everyone has a life of their own and should not be asked to sacrifice their own well-being for the sake of their family. A similar proportion said they agreed equally with both statements (17 per cent). Pakistanis were more polarised in their views, with a quarter espousing an individualistic approach, but almost none agreeing equally with both statements.

VIEWS ON WOMEN AND PAID EMPLOYMENT

The family, then, has an importance to all the three South Asian groups and the desire to enhance family cohesion and the well-being of the family may well be a factor in business development. However, a key factor in how that development is shaped may be determined by the views held about women taking paid employment, and in particular about women working in the family business. As views might be different in respect of marital status, age and with whom the person worked, attitudes were explored in a number of ways.

Table 3.7   Attitudes of men towards married women doing paid work

percentage agreeing with the statement

	Indian	African Asian	Pakistani	All South Asians
Married women should have paid work if they want it	81	60	34	60
Married women should only have paid work if the family needs the money	8	30	17	18
Married women should spend their time looking after the home	11	10	48	23
Unweighted base	36	30	29	102

Male respondents were asked their views on married women working in the external labour market. Six out of ten of male South Asian entrepreneurs believed that married women should have paid work if they wanted it (Table 3.7). Less than a quarter (23 per cent) said that women should spend their time looking after the home and not work in the external labour market. However, these overall statistics mask important differences between the different ethnic groups: Indians (81 per cent) and

African Asians (60 per cent) were nearly twice to two and a half times as likely as Pakistanis (34 per cent) to state that married women should do paid work if they wanted it. Conversely, nearly half of Pakistani men reported they would like married women to spend their time looking after the home compared to only a tenth of Indians and African Asians. The data suggest that there is a clear demarcation between the views held by Indians and African Asians on women working in the external labour market and Pakistanis.

Table 3.8   Male attitudes towards married women working in the family business

	percentage agreeing with the statement			
	Indian	African Asian	Pakistani	All South Asians
Married women should work in the family business if they want to	79	58	39	62
Married women should only work in the family business if the family needs the money	16	32	14	17
Married women should spend their time looking after the home and not work in the family business	5	10	38	18
Unweighted base	38	31	28	103

This divide also holds true when respondents were asked about whether married women should be working in the family business (Table 3.8). Four-fifths of Indians and three-fifths of African Asians said that married women should work in the family business if they so desired, compared to two-fifths of Pakistanis. The same proportion of Pakistani men believed that married women should spend their time looking after the home and not work in the family business, compared to hardly any Indians or African Asians. So while married women doing paid work was not as such an issue among Indians and African Asians, Pakistanis were divided about it. The data strongly indicate that the critical factor in explaining this division of opinion between Indians and African Asians on the one hand and Pakistanis on the other was not the Pakistani entrepreneur's view that women should not work outside the family business, but that they should be doing paid work at all. Conversely, in the case of Indians and African Asians, there was no significant preference for married women working in either family-run businesses or elsewhere.

Only slightly more of the self-employed were happy to have their daughters working in their business, than had been to have their wives (Table 3.9). The pattern across ethnic groups was similar to attitudes towards wives working, with a high proportion of Pakistani entrepreneurs not wishing their daughters to work in the family business: twice as many Indians (86 per cent) and African Asians (71 per cent) were happy with their daughter working in the family business than Pakistanis (39 per cent). Conversely, three-fifths of Pakistani respondents reported they would be unhappy with their daughter working in the family business compared to only one in seven of Indians and just over a quarter of African Asians.

Table 3.9   Male attitudes towards daughter working in the family
             business

			column percentages
	Indian	African Asian	Pakistani	All South Asians
Happy	86	71	39	66
Unweighted base	28	24	28	86

A set of questions were asked of the respondents which sought to ascertain the degree to which views on women working were shaped by with whom they might work. These series of questions consistently revealed major differences between Indians and African Asians on the one hand, and Pakistanis on the other, over the preferred role for their daughter in the labour market (Table 3.10). Almost all the Indian and four-fifths of African Asian respondents preferred their daughters to be working in businesses which employed men and women from white and other ethnic minority groups, whereas the largest proportion of Pakistanis preferred their daughters working in businesses which employed either only women from their own ethnic group (65 per cent), or businesses which employed women from white and other ethnic minority groups as well (64 per cent). The concern seems to be the mixing of the sexes rather than the mixing of groups.

Table 3.10 Proportion of men happy for daughter working, by gender and ethnicity of colleagues*

column percentages

	Indian	African Asian	Pakistani	All South Asians
Women only, own ethnic group	68	54	65	64
Women only, own religious group	72	45	58	60
Women and men, own ethnic group	68	65	33	51
Women and men, own religious group	72	41	33	48
Women only, all ethnic groups	96	74	64	79
Women and men, all ethnic groups	97	83	30	69
*Unweighted base**	*28*	*24*	*28*	*86*

*   Respondents were asked to say whether they would be very happy, fairly happy, fairly unhappy or very unhappy: the first two have been grouped and reported as 'happy'.
** Base varied slightly across questions.

Looking at each ethnic group in detail, the hierarchy was as follows. Indians were happiest for their daughters to work in mixed ethnicity workplaces and were equally happy with women only or mixed gender workplaces; for them segregation to their own ethnic group or to their own religious group was equally least favoured. African Asians similarly preferred mixed ethnicity workplaces; they also preferred mixed gender and were least keen on workplaces with employees limited to their own religion. In the case of Pakistanis, the results of these series of questions were markedly different. Gender played a critical role in the types of workplaces that the Pakistani respondents wished their daughters to work in, and it was within such a context that cultural factors such as religion may potentially act as a constraint on maximising opportunities in the labour market. Pakistani respondents were least happy with their daughters working in mixed sex workplaces. It did not matter to them whether the businesses employed men from the same ethnic group, or from the same religious group, or from white and other ethnic minority groups. The issue for them was clearly one to do with the separation of sexes, rather than one of ethnic or religious exclusivity.

The data, therefore, indicate strongly that Indians and African Asians had little objection to, and indeed appeared to prefer their daughters working in businesses where men and women from both white and other ethnic minority groups worked. On the other hand, Pakistani respondents preferred their daughters not to be working at all. If there was no choice and they had to work, they were most happy with them working in businesses which employed only women, irrespective of their ethnic origin or religion. These differences between the various ethnic groups will be important as we go on to discuss what this means in relation to South Asian business development.

ATTITUDES TOWARDS RISK AND SUCCESS

Risk-taking may be seen as an inevitable part of establishing and running a business and approaches to risk may affect business success. Risk was explored in a number of ways in the study. Firstly, the degree of conservatism was explored. Secondly, the degree to which individuals saw business success as inherently risky or whether it could be underwritten in some way was examined.

Table 3.11 Risk and conservatism

Respondents were presented with two pairs of statements and asked which in each pair they most agreed with.

Statement A: *"It is better to be cautious about making major changes in life."*
Statement B: *"You will never achieve much unless you act boldly."*

				column percentages
	Indian	African Asian	Pakistani	All South Asians
Agreed most with Statement A	73	63	41	59
Agreed equally with both	8	23	10	16
Agreed most with Statement B	19	14	48	25
Unweighted base	*52*	*35*	*29*	*122*

Statement A: *"Ideas that have stood the test of time are generally better."*
Statement B: *"New ideas are generally better than old ones."*

Agreed most with Statement A	53	31	39	41
Agreed equally with both	27	25	10	25
Agreed most with Statement B	20	44	52	34
Unweighted base	*51*	*36*	*31*	*122*

Tables 3.11 and 3.12 seek to establish to what degree our sample of South Asian business owners were risk-takers and were willing to take bold decisions. Table 3.11 appears to suggest that a greater proportion of Indians (73 per cent) and African Asians (63 per cent) were likely to be cautious in deciding to make major changes in their lives than Pakistanis (41 per cent). Conversely, Pakistani business owners revealed more boldness in their attitudes with almost half (48 per cent) of them agreeing with the statement that you never achieve much unless you act boldly, compared to only one in five of Indians (19 per cent) and one in seven of African Asians (14 per cent) who agreed with this statement. It may be that the Indians and African Asians were expressing a cautiousness that is fairly typical of the self-employed (it was found among the Edinburgh shopkeepers in

Bechhofer et al, 1974), and that it is the Pakistanis that are anomalous. A question about the relative merits of new and old ideas confirmed a more cautious approach among Indians, with 53 per cent agreeing strongly that ideas which have stood the test of time were generally better, and less caution among Pakistanis (of whom over half felt that new ideas were better than old ones). However, African Asians did not exhibit the same caution over new ideas, reflecting a similar attitude to Pakistanis, with a greater proportion favouring new ideas.

Associated with risk and attitudes to change is the degree to which individuals feel in control over their business, and success is achievable. Issues of control and success were explored in a series of questions about what makes a successful business, including to what extent business success was attributed to personal skill and hard work compared to more metaphysical beliefs such as God's will (Tables 3.12 to 3.17).

The study found that most Indian, African Asian and Pakistani business owners attributed business success to a combination of factors including an individual's personal skills and hard work (85 per cent); God's will (67 per cent); and good luck (56 per cent). Smaller proportions also attributed business success to help from other people (34 per cent); spiritual merit from one's actions in this life (23 per cent); and spiritual merit through actions in a previous life (15 per cent).

Tables 3.12 - 3.17

Business success results from a person's skills and hard work

	Indian	African Asian	Pakistani	All South Asians
	*percentage agreeing with the statement**			
A great deal	89	81	82	85
A little	11	19	18	15

Business success results from help from other people

	Indian	African Asian	Pakistani	All South Asians
	*percentage agreeing with the statement**			
A great deal	38	39	25	34
A little	57	50	72	59

Business success results from good luck

	*percentage agreeing with the statement**		
A great deal	57	50	65	56
A little	40	47	29	39

Business success results from spiritual merit through one's actions in this life

	*percentage agreeing with the statement**		
A great deal	15	24	32	23
A little	38	35	23	33

Business success results from spiritual merit through actions in a previous life

	*percentage agreeing with the statement**		
A great deal	14	21	16	15
A little	34	21	9	23

Business success results from God's will

	*percentage agreeing with the statement**		
A great deal	66	43	94	67
A little	32	37	3	25
Unweighted base	*53*	*36*	*33*	*129***

* The 'not at all' response has been allowed for in calculating the displayed figures but is not included in the table.
** The base varied between questions.

Most difference between ethnic groups appeared to relate to religion. Nearly all Pakistanis (94 per cent) attributed business success directly to God's will and one third attributed it to spiritual merit in one's actions in this life. This compares with 66 per cent of Indians and 43 per cent of African Asians attributing success to God's will, and 15 per cent of Indians and 24 per cent of African Asians attributing it to spiritual merit of actions in this life. While few of any group thought that business success resulted, a great deal, from the spiritual merit of their actions in a previous life, over 40 per cent of Indians and African Asians felt this contributed in some degree to business success. Similar proportions of each ethnic group considered success to result from hard work. However, more Pakistanis than Indians attributed a greater role to luck, and Indians and African Asians were more inclined than Pakistanis to attribute help from other people as contributing to business success.

Thus, while all ethnic groups similarly attributed business success to hard work, and therefore considered individuals to have some control over outcomes, more Pakistanis than Indians and African Asians seemed to believe success depended on how God looked upon them. It is difficult to know how exactly to interpret the significance of this for the differences in self-employment between the Pakistanis and the others. Given the importance, that the Pakistanis said, of religion to how they lived (which was consistent with the findings of the Fourth Survey), their belief in their economic dependence on God has to be taken seriously. In fact, it has the potential at least partly to explain an anomaly. We have seen in this chapter that Pakistanis do not just emphasise the importance of religion but are considerably more conservative on the question of women working than African Asians and Indians. Pakistanis and Bangladeshis (both predominantly Muslim groups) were also found to be more culturally conservative than their South Asian peers in a study of intergenerational identity changes (Modood, Beishon and Virdee, 1994).

A quantitative analysis of cultural conservatism is also offered in the context of the findings of the Fourth Survey (Modood et al, 1997). It is argued there, by reference to a number of cultural variables such as religion, language and marriage, and controlling for factors such as age and length of residence in Britain, that Pakistanis are distinctly more culturally retentive than the African Asians and Indians (Modood et al, 1997). Yet, as we have also seen in this chapter, the Pakistani self-employed were the least likely in our sample to have conservative attitudes in relation to risk and trying out new ideas. The anomaly, therefore, is how is it that what seems to be the most culturally conservative group seems to be the most bold and open in relation to economic activity. This anomaly is reinforced by the consideration that, as we shall see in the next chapter, in terms of human capital – education, experience, skills – the help of others, market analysis, planning and access to capital, the Pakistanis are not well placed compared to the other Asian groups.

Part of the explanation for the anomalously high rate of Pakistani self-employment must lie in the 'push' factors that were discussed in Chapter 2, the poor prospects for pay and promotion of those in work, the higher rates of unemployment and the experience of racism. But it may also be that individuals who believe that their success or failure is dependent upon divine providence have less reason to be cautious. Those who believe that God will look after and reward those who abide by his commandments have a reason to be religiously conservative and economically optimistic simultaneously. The economic morale of Pakistanis and other Muslims may, therefore, be critically linked to their religious faith and practice, which may be a source of economic self-confidence greater than can be justified by purely economic or human capital analyses.

The Pakistani self-employed on this analysis are an important counter-example to certain sociological analyses of modern (or, as it is sometimes called, 'late modern' or 'post-modern') society. For contemporary society has been characterised as one of heightened risk and uncertainty (Beck, Giddens and Lash, 1994; Gidddens, 1994), and it is said that for individuals to flourish they need to embrace uncertainty (Baumann, 1996). The risk-taking Pakistanis in this study, however, seemed to be born of a mixture of economic insecurity and religious faith, with the latter providing a sense of security from which risk could be faced. It is a sense of security that is tied to a conception of justice. In the explanation of Muslim views on usury and interest-taking, it was pointed out that the sharing of risk was seen as critical to just financial transactions. It has been said that 'the crux of the argument is that profit is legitimate only as a reward for risk' (Kuran, 1995:227). On this view, it could be said that to call oneself a businessman or businesswoman and yet seek to avoid business risk is to try to limit one's dependence on God. The Muslims in our survey who attribute business success to God's will can perhaps be compared to Weber's Protestants, who developed an entrepreneurial ethic based upon the ideas of predestination and that God will look after those who are God-fearing but economically aspiring (Weber, 1930; see also Tawney, 1926). It appears that for these Muslims religion is not a relic from pre-modern times nor a matter of private feeling. It is a collectively nourished psychological asset that is not just relevant to business conduct but relevant to economic success or failure. If we have interpreted this correctly, it may help to explain why some Muslims, as in *The Satanic Verses* affair, are so sensitive of representations that belittle their religion and so threaten a basis of their well-being (Modood, 1990 and 1993).

TRUST

Some of the approaches to explaining the development of ethnic businesses have focused on networks between people from the same ethnic group (Waldinger et al, 1990). Ethnic groups may be important in helping to explain successful entrepreneurial activity both in terms of which groups of people business is conducted with and in terms of identification of markets, suppliers, credit and so on. An important element of this is the degree to which different groups are trusted. This is explored below.

Table 3.18 Can people be trusted?

	Indian	African Asian	Pakistani	All South Asians
				column percentages
Most people can be trusted	38	44	32	38
You can't be too careful in dealing with people	57	42	65	52
Agree equally with both statements	6	14	3	10
Unweighted base	*53*	*36*	*31*	*127*

In general, most of the self-employed were cautious about trusting people (62 per cent felt you could not be too careful in dealing with people), although almost half (48 per cent) felt that most people could be trusted (Table 3.18). Pakistanis seemed to be most cautious and African Asians most prone to trust people.

Almost two-fifths of the self-employed in the study declared that who could be trusted affected their business (Table 3.19). African Asians were less likely than other groups to see this as an issue and Pakistanis most likely. As the business of a significant minority was affected, it was important to explore in more detail who could be trusted.

Table 3.19   Trust affects business

				column percentages
	Indian	African Asian	Pakistani	All South Asians
Who can be trusted affects business	40	28	47	38
Unweighted base	*53*	*36*	*32*	*128*

Certain groups of people were seen to be more trustworthy in general than others, which might affect the role of different groups in the businesses of South Asians. The study found that nearly all (94 per cent) South Asian business owners in this sample said they could always or usually trust their own family (Table 3.20). A further two-thirds (67 per cent) of all South Asian business owners reported that people from their own religious group could nearly always be trusted. However, the overall results masked some important differences between the different ethnic groups and who they believed they could normally trust. Just over two-fifths (43 per cent) of Pakistanis said they normally trusted British people compared to almost two-thirds (63 per cent) who said they normally trusted Asian people. On the other hand, Indians were equally likely to report that they normally trusted British people (57 per cent), Asians (57 per cent) and people from the same country of origin (57 per cent). About half of the African Asian business owners said they could nearly always trust British people (50 per cent), Asians (47 per cent) and people from the same country of origin (52 per cent).

Table 3.20 Who can usually be trusted?

column percentages

	Indian	African Asian	Pakistani	All South Asians
Family	95	97	96	94
Own religious group	64	69	67	67
Same country of origin	57	52	48	52
Asian people	57	47	63	55
British people	57	50	43	52
Unweighted base	52	35	29	122

The data, then, appear to suggest that South Asian business owners were more likely normally to trust people who were members of their own family. This seems to be consistent with research perspectives that emphasise the family as a uniquely important unit for cooperative enterprise (Sanders and Nee, 1996; Afshar, 1989). What is more novel in the answers of respondents is the degree of trust reposed in co-religionists in preference to members of other groups to which one may belong, such as persons of one's own ethnic or national origins. Pakistanis once again differed somewhat from the other groups, though it is not clear why. Pakistanis said they were more likely to trust fellow Asians than fellow-Pakistanis, and British people least so. On the other hand, Indians and African Asians were about as likely to trust people of the same origins, fellow Asians and white Britons; indeed, among Indians even the preference for co-religionists was slight, whereas it was clearly a strong preference among African Asians and Pakistanis. Given the greater proportion of Pakistanis and, to a slightly lesser extent, Indians, who said that who they trusted affected their business, one would expect Pakistani businesses to a greater extent to be located in the family and among co-religionists and also in networks of Asians.

SUMMARY AND CONCLUSION

Following on from previous research which has identified the importance of cultural factors in self-employment, this chapter has identified a number of cultural factors among the sample which may affect the development of the business. It has found no support for the view that the self-employed are steeped in a moral and political individualism. It has, however, found significant differences among South Asian groups.

In terms of family background potentially providing knowledge, assistance or encouragement for self-employment, the sample was well served. Half had a family history of self-employment and about one fifth had had relatives in a similar line of business to their own. On the other hand, fewer had actually worked in the family business. African Asians seemed to have the edge over other groups in terms of their background, although a high proportion of Pakistanis had a family history of self-employment and a fifth of Indians had worked in a family business.

Family and work were very important to the self-employed and most placed more emphasis on the family than the individual. A fifth of the Indians and African Asians placed equal emphasis upon the family and the individual, but the Pakistanis were more inclined to choose either one or the other. The sample were not strongly risk orientated. Pakistanis were less averse to risk and more open to new ideas, while Indians seemed the most cautious and conservative group. African Asians were risk averse but open to new ideas. Other differences were apparent in general outlook on life, with leisure and friends seeming to assume more importance to Indians than to other groups.

As the family business has been seen as a vehicle for family cohesion, views on women and employment may be an important influence on self-employment. Self-employment seemed to offer more opportunities for family cohesion (at least in relation to women) for Indians, in particular, and African Asians than for Pakistanis, as many of the latter were not keen on their female relatives working in the family business. Indeed, in relation to married women, many Pakistanis did not believe they should have employment at all. However, the influence of these views on self-employment and the business may have been reduced because most Indians and many African Asians were equally happy for women to work outside as well as within the family business.

Religion was important to three-quarters of the self-employed and, as such, was likely to influence people's general approach to life and hence their business approach. However, variation was likely over ethnic groups, as religious affiliation varied: all Pakistanis were Muslim; a substantial minority of Indians were not religious, while the majority of the remainder were mainly Hindu or Sikh; most African Asians were also Hindu or Sikh, but about one quarter were Muslim, Christian or Jain. For Pakistanis, in particular, the scope for religion directly affecting business was apparent, due to proscriptions for Muslims in handling various products and in borrowing with interest.

Religion also appeared to shape people's beliefs about the sources of success in business. Nearly all attributed to themselves some responsibility for success, either directly (as all did) to their own hard work or indirectly (as about half of each group did) to spiritual merit from one's own actions. However, nearly all Pakistanis, more than for any other group, also attributed success to God's will. Paradoxically, these views may have been linked to attitudes towards risk and innovation described above: if one believes that God will reward the virtuous and hard-working one has a reason simultaneously to be more confident about economic outcomes while being religiously conservative.

Finally, there was evidence that trust was likely to affect the development of the business in ways which were family, religion or ethnicity based, but that the approach differed across the ethnic groups. Not surprisingly, for all groups, this was likely to favour business involvement with other members of the family. Otherwise, about two-thirds tended to favour their own religious group, with Pakistanis also favouring Asian people in general. Indians did not seem to trust any one group, other than their family, more than another.

Thus there appears to be substantial circumstantial evidence that cultural factors may shape self-employment for South Asians and lead to different patterns of business development. The next three chapters explore this further by linking these cultural factors with entry, development of and success in business.

Note
1   A broader discussion of these issues is included in Modood et al, 1997.

Chapter 4

STARTING UP IN BUSINESS

This chapter examines a range of issues around entry into self-employment: the motivation for self-employment, the choice of business and the process of setting up in business. It examines the resources to which individuals had access and the difficulties encountered. In particular, the chapter evaluates the claims of two sometimes conflicting approaches to understanding South Asian entry into business: the first, which alleges that entry into business is primarily motivated by the constraints that visible minorities are faced with in the external labour market (Aldrich et al, 1981; Ram, 1992; Jones et al, 1994); and the second approach which stresses the importance of cultural factors in determining entry into business (Werbner, 1990a and 1990b; Waldinger et al, 1990; Srinivasan, 1992 and 1995). This chapter adopts an interactive approach to these conflicting theories on understanding entry into business, and seeks to establish the relative degree of weight that this sample of South Asian entrepreneurs themselves attach to what motivated them to enter business.

ENTRY INTO SELF-EMPLOYMENT

South Asian self-employment took off in the latter part of the 1970s and this is reflected in our sample, most of whom started in business in the 1980s (Table 4.1). Over 70 per cent had started in business before 1990 and over 40 per cent prior to 1985. There was some variation across ethnic groups in when self-employment had first become a main economic activity: for most African Asians this had occurred in the 1980s, whilst Pakistanis, comparatively, had entered in two waves, before the 1980s and after the 1980s.[1]

Table 4.1   The year self-employment became the main job, by ethnic group

				column percentages
	Indian	African Asian	Pakistani	All South Asians
1964 - 1969	2	3	0	2
1970 - 1974	6	3	9	6
1975 - 1979	14	6	18	13
1980 - 1984	22	33	9	22
1985 - 1989	30	31	21	29
1990 - 1994	26	25	42	29
Unweighted base	*51*	*36*	*33*	*126*

Entry into self-employment may be complex: people may start by running a business part-time, whilst holding down a job, and people may move in and out of self-employment; they may buy a business, start a business, move into partnership; and their business may be singly or jointly owned. For this sample, the process of entry to self-employment tended to be straightforward: individuals moved directly into self-employment as a full-time activity and most then stayed self-employed; they tended to start the business themselves and to be sole owners.

Ninety-five per cent of their first experience of self-employment for the self-employed was when they started to run their own business full-time: only 5 per cent went into self-employment more gradually by running a business part-time before it became their main job (Table 4.2).[2] Almost none had had experience of running a business part-time and, although 16 per cent may have gained some experience through working in a family-owned business, for most, such experience was short-lived (see

Chapter 3). Thus, nearly all the sample lacked self-employment experience when they set up in business full-time.

Table 4.2   Past experience of running a business before it became the main job

			column percentages
	Indian	African Asian	Pakistani	All South Asians
Ran a business before it became their main job	4	0	6	5
The business was the main job as soon as they started running it	96	100	94	95
Unweighted base	*53*	*36*	*33*	*129*

Given this lack of experience, it was not surprising that, at first entry to full-time self-employment, almost everyone owned a single business only. One person alone owned more than one (owning two businesses) when they first moved into self-employment full-time.

Table 4.3   The ways in which respondents entered self-employment

			column percentages
	Indian	African Asian	Pakistani	All South Asians
Started the business themselves	47	64	67	57
Took over operating business	38	28	15	28
Became a partner	13	6	6	10
Inherited the business	0	0	0	0
Other	2	3	12	5
Unweighted base	*53*	*36*	*33*	*129*

A large proportion of the businesses owned by our sample were started by the respondents themselves (57 per cent). This is a particularly risky approach to self-employment. However, a significant minority of the sample had either taken over an operating business (28 per cent) or had become a partner in an existing business (10 per cent). There was some difference between the three main ethnic minority groups, with a greater proportion of African Asians (64 per cent) and Pakistanis (67 per cent) having started the business themselves than Indian respondents (47 per cent). Conversely, Indians were more likely to have taken over an existing business (38 per cent) than Pakistanis (15 per cent).

When they first started in business, most people went into business alone. Twice as many were sole owners of their business (67 per cent) than shared the ownership of the business (33 per cent) (Table 4.4). Indians were more likely than African Asians and Pakistanis to start in business with other people.

Table 4.4   Business start-up: ownership

				column percentages
	Indian	African Asian	Pakistani	All South Asians
Sole owner	58	72	73	66
One co-owner: family	21	11	9	14
Co-owners: all family	15	11	9	12
Co-owners: family and non-family	0	3		1
Co-owners: all non-family	6	3	6	6
One co-owner: non-family	0	0	3	2
Unweighted base	*53*	*36*	*33*	*129*

Family played a major role in shared ownership. For those that shared ownership, 75 per cent (26 per cent of the total sample) were in business with members of their family only, and a further 2 per cent (1 per cent of the whole sample) were in business with both family and non-family members. Family co-owners were usually close family members: of those that shared the business with at least one family member, most shared with their spouse (61 per cent, 16 per cent of the whole sample), 36 per cent (9 per cent of the whole sample) shared with their brother or brother-in-law, and a small proportion shared with their father (or father-in-law), mother (or mother-in-law) cousin or another relative.

Twenty-seven per cent of those that shared ownership (10 per cent of the whole sample) started in business with non-family co-owners and nearly all of these had no family co-owners. Non-family co-owners tended to be either South Asian or white. Owing to the small numbers involved, it was not possible to determine whether there was a tendency for people to have partners from their own ethnic group.

Because of the greater tendency among all groups for those in partnership to be in partnership with family members, and because of Indians' greater tendency to be in partnership, Indian businesses were more likely to be run by a family (rather than by an individual or a partnership involving non-family members): 36 per cent of Indians compared with 22 per cent of African Asians and 18 per cent of Pakistanis. This partly reflects the fact that a larger proportion of Indian women were self-employed (Table 2.3), women being more likely to have a husband as a partner, and that a large minority of Pakistani men were opposed to their wives working in the family business, and a large minority of African Asians gave the idea only limited support (Table 3.8).

ACCESS TO CAPITAL

An important constraint to starting up in business is access to sufficient capital. This survey asked respondents how they had financed their business venture, especially the sources they had used to start up (Table 4.5).

About a sixth (15 per cent) of the total sample did not require any funds to finance the business. However, we do not know whether this was because they had sufficient funds to set up in business or that the business venture required no initial capital outlay. For those who did require finance to start their business up, the most common sources of funds were personal savings (68 per cent), the bank (42 per cent) and loans from family (23 per cent) and friends (18 per cent). Family assistance mainly stopped short of gifts and few accessed other forms of formal loans such as those from loan companies. Few had received financial assistance from a governmental body or enterprise agency, though Pakistanis were most likely to.

Table 4.5   The ways in which the business was financed

column percentages

	Indian	African Asian	Pakistani	All South Asians
No funds needed	17	26	3	15
Unweighted base	*52*	*35*	*31*	*125*
Of those that required funds				
Savings	72	69	53	68
Bank	53	31	30	42
Loans from family	19	27	30	23
Loans from friends	19	23	13	18
Loan/grant from government/local authority/ enterprise agency	2	8	13	7
Mortgage	7	8	3	6
Loan company	0	4	0	1
Gift from family	0	8	0	3
Inheritance	0	0	3	1
Redundancy pay	0	0	3	1
Other	9	15	13	11
Unweighted base	*43*	*26*	*30*	*106*

There was some difference across the various South Asian groups: a quarter of African Asians (26 per cent) and a sixth of Indians (17 per cent) reported they had not needed any funds to set up in business compared to only 3 per cent of Pakistanis. Indians and African Asians seemed to have more of their own resources to call upon, with more Indians (72 per cent) and

African Asians (69 per cent) reported utilising their personal savings than Pakistanis (53 per cent). Indians, too, seemed to have better access to formal money markets with 53 per cent securing finance from a bank, compared with 31 per cent of African Asians and 30 per cent of Pakistanis. On the other hand, African Asians (35 per cent) and Pakistanis (33 per cent) had more support from their families than Indians (19 per cent).

Religious beliefs may have played a part in shaping this pattern. As we saw in Chapter 3, three-quarters of Pakistanis, 15 per cent of African Asians and 2 per cent of Indians said their religion had a view on the lending or borrowing of money for interest (all of these were Muslim). Over one quarter of Pakistanis reported that their religious beliefs had affected their access to borrowing (either whether they borrowed or how they borrowed money), whereas borrowing was affected by religious beliefs for only 2 per cent of Indians and 3 per cent of African Asians (Table 4.6). Although respondents were not asked to confine their response to start-up funding, it seems likely that religion played a part in the pattern of borrowing by Pakistanis, with greater borrowing from relatives and less through banks.

Table 4.6 Religious beliefs and access to capital

			percentage of each ethnic group
	Indian	African Asian	Pakistani	All South Asians
Religion has a view on the borrowing/ lending for interest	2	15	75	28
View has affected whether or how borrowed	2	3	28	11
No effect: not needed/ wanted to borrow	0	12	31	11
Could not say	0	0	16	5
Unweighted base	*51*	*34*	*32*	*123*

It is also possible that differential stereotyping by institutional lenders may have shaped this pattern. A study has found, for example, that 'Muslims were perceived to provide inferior information compared to Sikhs and Hindus by a number of bank managers and this affected treatment of propositions' (Deakins, Hussain and Ram, 1995:97). While our study did not directly explore this topic, other research does show that different groups of non-white people are stereotyped differently, and that various forms of prejudice and racism are directed at people not just on the basis of their non-European appearance but also on the basis of what are perceived to be distinctive cultural characteristics (Modood, 1996).

A small proportion, a fifth, had had problems in raising the money required to start up their business (Table 4.7).[3] Indians were least likely to encounter problems (10 per cent of the whole sample, 11 per cent of those needing finance), whereas a high proportion of African Asians encountered problems. African Asians were least likely to need to raise finance, but, when they did most often had difficulties. The most common problem in raising finance was not being able to find a guarantor for a loan (14 out of 22). Other problems (raised by a maximum of five people each) were over having one's own security; developing and having a business plan accepted; and partners failing to raise the necessary funds. Only one person said there was a problem due to needing a Muslim moneylender.

Table 4.7 Problems in raising money when starting the business

				column percentages
	Indian	African Asian	Pakistani	All South Asians
Proportion of whole sample	10	23	19	18
Unweighted base	*52*	*35*	*31*	*125*
Proportion of those requiring finance	11	32	20	21
Unweighted base	*44*	*25*	*30*	*105*

It seems, therefore, that Pakistanis were most in need of funds, were least likely to rely on savings but were most affected by religion, and possibly also by commercial institutional lenders' perceptions, in getting access to start-up capital. Their greater use of government, local authority and enterprise agency funding may be related to their difficulties with commercial lenders. African Asians had had the most difficulty in actually raising the money they sought, the main problem being able to find a guarantor for the loan. It is not clear why they as a group should have had a greater problem than other groups, though possibly it may be that they requested larger loans.

TYPE OF BUSINESS

The self-employed entered a narrow range of industries (Table 4.7). A high proportion went into retailing (42 per cent), with nearly all the remainder going into artisan-style services (18 per cent), restaurants (12 per cent), cab driving (9 per cent) and a small range of other types of services (13 per cent). Only 6 per cent went into manufacturing, all of whom ran clothing businesses.

There was considerable variation in the line of business that different ethnic minority groups entered. Indians and Pakistanis tended to be concentrated in one or two industries, whilst the African Asian self-employed were spread over a wider range of business ventures. Half the Indians were involved in retail, with most either running grocery/off licence shops or newsagents; two-thirds of the Pakistani business owners were engaged in retailing (particularly running grocery/off licence shops) or in running their own cab firms; whereas African Asians were evenly distributed in businesses such as newsagents, restaurants, clothes retailers, carpentry, building and car repairs. This is broadly consistent with the original, larger sample of the Fourth Survey except that in the latter, half of each of these three Asian groups were in retail, fewer were in artisan-based services and one in five of the African Asians were in financial services (Modood et al, 1997).

Table 4.8 Industry of initial business

percentage of each ethnic group

	Indian	African Asian	Pakistani	All South Asians
Retail	51	32	42	42
Grocery/off licence	15	6	27	16
Newsagents	19	9	3	11
Clothes retailer	8	9	3	6
TV/video retailer	4	0	6	3
Household goods	6	9	3	6
Restaurants	8	9	9	12
Artisan-based services	15	35	6	18
Building	6	9	3	6
Car repair	6	9	3	6
Carpenter	2	15	0	5
Other skilled workers (eg plumbers)	2	3	0	2
Other services	17	21	36	22
Cab drivers	8	0	24	9
Insurance sales	2	6	0	2
Driving instructor	2	9	3	4
Professional (eg dentist, accountant)	0	3	9	3
Other	3	3	0	3
Clothing manufacture	9	3	6	6
Unweighted base	*53*	*34*	*33*	*127*

Many factors may influence the choice of initial business. Individuals may make well-informed choices based on markets and opportunities; they may choose a particular line because it uses their job-specific skills and knowledge; they may be assisted or encouraged into a particular line by family and friends with knowledge of an industry, particularly through their own self-employment in the industry; and chance, such as a business for sale, may affect choice. Furthermore, capital needs and access to capital may constrain business possibilities and, as we have already seen, religious beliefs may affect possibilities (see Chapter 3).

Respondents were asked for their reasons for entering their particular line of business (Table 4.9). The choice of type of business was more often related to encouragement by family or friends in a similar business (33 per cent) and seeing a market opportunity (29 per cent) than other factors. However, about a fifth said the business was for sale (20 per cent); or they had been working in a similar business (16 per cent) or had the relevant technical/professional skills (18 per cent).

Table 4.9   Reasons for choice of type of business

	Indian	African Asian	Pakistani	All South Asians
Encouraged by family or friends in similar businesses	32	31	41	33
Saw market opportunity	30	33	22	29
Business was for sale	36	17	9	20
Had the relevant technical professional skills	15	25	13	18
Had been working in similar businesses	4	31	13	16
Other	17	22	38	23
Unweighted base	*53*	*36*	*32*	*128*

Cell percentages do not always equal 100 per cent because the respondents could select more than one reason.

Some differences emerged when comparison was made across the various minority groups. Specifically, Indians and African Asians appeared to be more 'entrepreneurial' than the Pakistanis and appeared to set about strategically identifying a market opportunity and planning their entry into a particular line of business (30 and 33 per cent respectively), whereas only a fifth of Pakistanis had chosen their line of business due to identifying a market opportunity (22 per cent). The importance of family and friends was evident, with around a third of all the groups reported receiving encouragement from friends and family working in similar lines of business. African Asians were more likely to move into businesses which used their technical and professional skills (25 per cent) than Indians (15 per cent) or Pakistanis (13 per cent). Similarly, a much greater proportion of African Asians (31 per cent) had worked in similar businesses than Indians (4 per cent) or Pakistanis (13 per cent).

Capital issues, whilst not mentioned as affecting choice, seem to have underlain the type of business entered. All the businesses were low in capital intensity and therefore had relatively low capital barriers to entry. However, different considerations seemed to interact for different ethnic groups. African Asians, a group which contained both the highest proportion with no need to raise finance and also the highest proportion experiencing problems raising finance, were concentrated in artisan-based businesses, which have among the lowest capital costs but rely on the possession of job-specific skills. Owing to the skill requirements, these types of business were not open to many of the other individuals. Instead, whilst entering other relatively low capital cost businesses (for example, retail and cab driving), low entry cost, family and friends in similar businesses had a relatively greater influence.

Moreover, some groups went into business on a more secure footing than others. African Asians seemed better prepared in terms of relevant skills, including business experience, although Indians also seemed to exhibit an entrepreneurial flair in terms of being influenced by market opportunities. On the other hand, Pakistani entry into a particular line of business appeared to be less well planned, with few reporting they had the appropriate technical or professional skills necessary to succeed in a particular line of business or having had past experience in a similar line of business. All the minority groups reported receiving strong encouragement from friends and family in similar lines of business and, for Pakistanis at least, this was the most important factor why they chose to go into a particular line of business.

PREPARATION FOR BUSINESS

Although only about one sixth said their choice of business was influenced by their technical or professional skills or by working in a similar business, rather more felt they had acquired skills and knowledge in employment which had prepared them for their own business (Table 4.10). Thirty-nine per cent had been employed at some time before entering self-employment in a job which they felt had been helpful to their business. This was more common for African Asians (47 per cent) than Pakistanis (36 per cent) or Indians (28 per cent).

Table 4.10 The ways in which jobs were helpful when going into business

				column percentages
	Indian	African Asian	Pakistani	All South Asians
Acquired management skills	4	19	6	10
Acquired professional and technical skills	8	19	9	13
Acquired business skills	11	17	9	16
Made business contacts	2	14	13	8
Provided business ideas	4	8	6	6
Provided money to help buy the business	6	8	6	8
Provided contacts with potential customers	2	8	13	7
Other	8	6	6	6
All who said previous employment was helpful	28	47	36	39
Unweighted base	*53*	*36*	*33*	*129*

The way that employment had helped took a number of forms. The most common way in which a previous job had been helpful was in providing relevant skills: management skills (10 per cent of all respondents); professional/technical skills (13 per cent); and business skills (16 per cent). Reflecting the greater proportion of African Asians whose professional and technical skills had affected their choice of business, African Asians were more likely to report having developed professional or technical skills in their previous employment which were of use in self-employment (19 per cent, compared with 8 per cent of Indians and 6 per cent of Pakistanis). However, African Asians were also more likely to report having developed managerial and business skills which were of use (19 per cent and 17 per cent, respectively, compared with 4 per cent and 11 per cent of Indians for each skill respectively and 6 per cent and 9 per cent respectively of Pakistanis).

Another important potential benefit from previous employment was the development of business and customer contacts. Few of the self-employed benefited in this way: only 8 per cent had developed useful business contacts through their previous employment and 7 per cent had developed customer contacts. However, previous employment was more useful to African Asians and Pakistanis in this way, with 14 per cent and 13 per cent respectively reporting developing business contacts compared with 2 per cent of Indians, and 8 per cent and 13 per cent respectively developing customer contacts compared with 2 per cent of Indians. Previous employment helped a very small number in other ways, including providing money to buy the business (8 per cent) and business ideas (6 per cent).

EMPLOYEES AND OTHERS HELPING IN THE BUSINESS

Whilst two-thirds of people set up in business on their own, as sole owners, the majority had at least one other person helping them in the business.[4] Sixty per cent had either employees or others (including co-owners) helping in the business (Table 4.11). Most of those with assistance had one or two others working in the business. The family played a large role in this, with almost half receiving assistance from family members (Table 4.12). Nearly 30 per cent had non-family assistance when they first started in business, although it was rare to use non-family employees or others without also having family assistance.

Table 4.11 **The number of people employed or helping in the business when it was first set up, by ethnic group**

				column percentages
	Indian	African Asian	Pakistani	All South Asians
None	31	53	47	40
One	21	17	13	17
Two	17	14	13	14
Three – Four	19	6	19	14
Five – Nine	6	3	3	7
Ten or more	6	8	3	7
Unweighted base	*52*	*36*	*32*	*127*

Table 4.12 **Family and non-family employed or helping in the business when it was first set up, by ethnic group**

				column percentages
	Indian	African Asian	Pakistani	All South Asians
No employees	31	53	47	40
Family only	38	33	28	32
Non-family only	13	3	16	15
Both	19	11	9	13
Some family	58	44	38	46
Some non-family	33	14	25	29
Unweighted base	*52*	*36*	*32*	*127*

Perhaps reflecting both the higher degree of co-ownership and family ownership (see above), Indians were more likely than other groups to have employees or others assisting in the business (69 per cent) and more likely to have family assistance (58 per cent). African Asians (53 per cent) and Pakistanis (47 per cent) were more likely than Indians (31 per cent) to be working on their own, without assistance. Both African Asians (44 per cent) and Pakistanis (38 per cent) were less likely to receive assistance from family than were Indians (58 per cent). However, Pakistanis (25 per cent) and Indians (33 per cent) used non-family employees/assistance to a greater extent than did African Asians (14 per cent). There was no difference in the numbers assisting in the business by ethnic group.

In total, 362 people, other than the owners themselves, worked (paid or unpaid) in the businesses. This gave an average of three people (plus the owner) per business over all businesses or five people (plus the owner) over those that had at least one helper.

Thus Indian businesses, at start-up, can be characterised as family concerns to a greater degree than either African Asian or Pakistani businesses, and rarely sole ventures; and African Asian businesses as rarely providing employment outside the family. Pakistani businesses occupied the middle ground between the two.

FACTORS MOTIVATING THE MOVE TO SELF-EMPLOYMENT

The evidence presented so far provides few clues to why these South Asians became self-employed. Some commentators have suggested that family networks play a major role in encouraging self-employment. We have already seen that about half the self-employed had had relatives who were self-employed (Chapter 3) and that many received encouragement to become self-employed from their family and friends. Other researchers have found that self-employment was less a positive choice than an escape from poor employment prospects in the wider labour market. Some of the evidence so far supports this: in the three years prior to becoming self-employed, 16 per cent had experienced at least one period of unemployment (see Chapter 2). Moreover, the types of business entered were generally low-level and unlikely (without significant expansion) to provide more than a low income.

This section first examines a range of reasons respondents gave for setting up in business. It then focuses on aspects of employment. Overall, the data suggest that a combination of factors, both 'pull' and 'push' factors, were important in determining whether this sample of South Asians entered into business, and that there were differences across ethnic groups.

Table 4.13 Reasons for setting up in business

	Indian	African Asian	Pakistani	All South Asians
				column percentages
Set up in business to increase income	52	83	72	68
Set up in business because wanted to be own boss	47	67	78	63
Set up in business to increase standing among family	25	44	53	39
Set up in business to increase standing among ethnic or religious community	15	22	25	21
Set up in business to increase standing among British society	21	31	25	26
Set up in business because local job opportunities were inadequate	30	47	63	45
Set up in business because job opportunities were in adequate because of racism	8	33	56	27
Set up in business because wanted to escape from racial harassment	8	25	40	20
Set up in business because I was unemployed	8	14	28	14
Unweighted base *	*53*	*36*	*33*	*129*

* Base varied slightly across questions.

Table 4.13 presents the reasons the self-employed gave for setting up in business. Two reasons for setting up in business were common to the majority of respondents: the desire to increase income (68 per cent) and a desire for independence, to be their own boss, (63 per cent). Both of these could be interpreted as either positive, pull factors: self-employment offering a good income and independence. Alternatively, they might result from poor employment prospects and conditions in the labour market.

Indeed, labour market problems in general (lack of adequate local job opportunities) were a push for almost half, although only 14 per cent said they entered business because they were unemployed. The experience of racial discrimination and racial harassment in the external labour market were important reasons for entering self-employment for between a quarter (27 per cent) and a fifth (20 per cent) respectively.

Self-employment was seen as conferring status by a large minority of respondents. About two-fifths of the self-employed said that they set up in business to increase their standing among the family (39 per cent). A smaller proportion said they set up in business because it would increase their standing within British society (26 per cent) and within their ethnic or religious community (21 per cent).

Of particular interest were the differences between ethnic groups and the relative importance given to push and pull factors in determining entry into business. For example, in the case of Pakistanis, almost two-thirds (63 per cent) said they set up in business because local job opportunities were inadequate. Aspects of inadequacy included racism (56 per cent); the desire to escape from racial harassment (40 per cent) and unemployment (28 per cent). Other aspects of labour market inadequacy are discussed below. Although it is difficult to separate out cause and effect, it does seem likely that such negative experiences in the wider labour market may also have contributed to them stating in such large proportions that they set up in business to be their own boss (78 per cent) and to increase their income (72 per cent).

On the other hand, a smaller (although still large) proportion of African Asians cited they set up in business because local job opportunities were inadequate (47 per cent). This lack of opportunity appears to be in part due to racism (33 per cent); the desire to escape racial harassment (25 per cent) and unemployment (14 per cent). Again, probably motivated in part by such a negative experience in the wider labour market, a large proportion of African Asian business owners said they set up in business to be their own boss (67 per cent) and to increase their income (83 per cent).

Indian business owners were least likely to report that their negative experiences in the wider labour market may have contributed to their decision to set up in business: even so, 30 per cent said they had set up in business because local job opportunities were inadequate. Moreover, a significantly smaller proportion were likely to attribute such negative experiences to racism, with only one in twelve stating that either racism (8 per cent) or the desire to escape from racial harassment (8 per cent) had been factors that had determined their entry into business. About half of the Indian sample said they had set up in business because they wanted to be their own boss (47 per cent) and because they wished to increase their income (52 per cent).

Chapter 4 showed that the three ethnic groups were similar in their attitude towards money. This lends support to the argument that the higher proportion of Pakistanis and African Asians compared with Indians who started in business to increase their income was due to poor labour market prospects as employees.

Another important difference to emerge in terms of understanding the motives for entry into self-employment was that African Asians were one and a half times as likely, and Pakistanis twice as likely (44 and 31 per cent and 53 per cent and 25 per cent respectively), to report they set up in business in order to increase their standing among their family than to increase their standing within British society. This contrasted with Indians who were far less motivated by status and almost equally likely to report that they had gone into business because of their desire to increase their standing within the community or within British society (25 per cent and 21 per cent respectively).

It appears that push factors such as the inadequacy of local job opportunities, in part due to the prevalence of racism and unemployment, were more important in the decision of Pakistani business owners to set up in business than for African Asians or Indians. Despite the, possibly negative, push factors that initially

forced these South Asians to consider self-employment, large proportions of all minority groups displayed a strong desire to be
their own boss and saw self-employment as a means of increasing
their income and sometimes increasing their status among their
own family. However, the greater negative experience in the
wider labour market may in part explain the reason why a substantial proportion of Pakistanis and a much lower proportion of
Indians stated they set up in business to be their own boss and
increase their income. In summary, pull factors associated with
autonomy and income seemed to be more important to Indians,
factors associated with standing and to a lesser extent the push of
unemployment and racism to African Asians, whilst the push of
unemployment and racism, and the pull of standing to a lesser
extent, were of more importance to Pakistanis.

EMPLOYMENT PRIOR TO ENTRY INTO SELF-EMPLOYMENT

A high proportion of the self-employed gave the 'inadequacy of
local job opportunities' as a reason for becoming self-employed.
This may cover a wide range of dissatisfactions: nature of job,
prospects and pay, for example. Unemployment was identified
separately above. This part of the chapter explores the degree to
which respondents were satisfied in the job they had immediately
prior to self-employment and with their employment prospects.

There appeared to be a high degree of dissatisfaction with
employment (Table 4.14). Almost one third were dissatisfied with
their employment prospects, half felt they were going nowhere,
half felt their skills and talents were not being used and 42 per
cent were worried about becoming unemployed. However, some
aspects of work were positive (or, at least, unproblematic) for
many. Pay was generally not a cause of dissatisfaction: 62 per
cent thought their pay prospects were reasonable, whilst only 15
per cent felt they were not. Whilst only one third said that their
work was fulfilling, only one fifth said that their work was posi-
tively not fulfilling. And half felt that they were building up their
skills and experience.

Table 4.14 Satisfaction with employment prior to self-employment

column percentages

	Indian	African Asian	Pakistani	All South Asians
I was satisfied with my employment prospects				
Agree	49	43	48	48
Disagree	23	34	42	31
I felt my skills and talents were not being used				
Agree	42	58	65	50
Disagree	32	14	19	25
I felt I was going nowhere				
Agree	38	53	77	52
Disagree	23	19	13	20
I felt I was building up skills and experience				
Agree	40	67	42	51
Disagree	21	14	35	21
I felt my pay prospects were reasonable				
Agree	55	69	65	62
Disagree	11	14	23	15
*I was worried about becoming unemployed**				
Agree	36	46	50	42
Disagree	26	29	38	30
*I found my work fulfilling**				
Agree	35	31	43	37
Disagree	22	26	17	22
*Unweighted base***	*53*	*36*	*31*	*127*

Respondents were asked to measure their agreement on a five-point scale. Those who neither agreed nor disagreed are not shown in the table.

* Only the employed were asked this question.

** Base varied between questions.

Some differences emerged between ethnic groups in their attitudes to employment preceding their entry into self-employment. On the whole, a greater proportion of Pakistanis were likely to report dissatisfaction than Indians or African Asians: 42 per cent were dissatisfied with their employment prospects, 65 per cent felt their skills were not being used and 77 per cent felt they were going nowhere. Comparative figures for Indians were 23 per cent, 42 per cent and 38 per cent respectively and, for African Asians, 34 per cent, 58 per cent and 53 per cent respectively.

Indians were less likely to be dissatisfied with aspects of their employment. However, satisfaction was more common among African Asians. A greater proportion of African Asians reported that, prior to self-employment, they were building up their skills and experience (67 per cent), whereas only two-fifths of Indians (40 per cent) and Pakistanis (42 per cent) felt they were building up their skills and experience. Pakistanis were most likely to disagree that they were building up their skills and experience.

There were some aspects of the job where all three minority groups were of a similar opinion: just under a half of Indians (49 per cent), African Asians (43 per cent) and Pakistanis (48 per cent) were satisfied with their employment prospects, and between a third and two-fifths of Indians (35 per cent), African Asians (31 per cent) and Pakistanis (43 per cent) found their work fulfilling.

SUMMARY AND CONCLUSION

There was strong evidence that both cultural and economic factors affected entry into self-employment. Substantial evidence was found of South Asians entering self-employment to escape a poor labour market and that racism was an integral experience of that labour market. However, positive features of self-employment also acted as a lure. Pull factors included a desire for autonomy, to improve income and to improve standing with others.

As a thrust to self-employment, economic factors impinged on the ethnic groups differently. Pakistanis were particularly prone to labour market difficulties, and racism was particularly widely experienced by this group. Many African Asians also complained of racism. Culturally, the promise of autonomy and an improved income seemed to be important to Indians, whereas improved status seemed more important to African Asians and Pakistanis. The desire to be one's own boss was also a major feature for Pakistanis, perhaps reflecting the more common desire among Pakistanis for independence identified in Chapter 3. However, it may also have been a case of labour market experience and cultural norms reinforcing each other.

Given this background, it was not surprising that start-up for most was not auspicious: most had no experience of self-employment when they started their first business and most started their business from scratch, although one quarter took over an existing business – more Indians than other groups – and 10 per cent entered through going into partnership in an existing business.

Economics also appeared to be at work in the choice and nature of the business. Whilst none of the self-employed mentioned capital constraints affecting their choice of business, it was noticeable that all entered business with low capital requirements. Indians seemed to have better personal access to capital, being able to draw on their own savings and on the formal money market, and few encountered problems raising finance. The lower use of formal money markets by the other two groups was noticeable, with African Asians tending to rely on personal savings, friends and family, and Pakistanis on family. As fewest Indians encountered problems in raising finance, this suggests a problem for African Asians and Pakistanis with accessing finance through banks. Religious beliefs may have played a role in this pattern, discouraging Muslims from seeking finance from banks.

Family and friends, too, were an influence on the choice of business and on its nature. About one third received encouragement to enter similar lines to that of family and friends. This was similar across groups. Most commonly, businesses were run entirely by the owner, without employees or other help. About one third had assistance from family members alone and about one quarter had non-family employees. Typically, the first business was under sole ownership. However, differences were apparent across ethnic groups. Indian businesses were least likely to be sole ventures and, at start-up, can be characterised as family concerns to a greater degree than African Asian or Pakistani businesses. Pakistani businesses were relatively more willing to employ non-family than family members. The low use of family ties in with the different attitudes between Pakistanis and Indians in respect of women working.

Other factors influencing choice of business suggested that different groups went into business on a more secure footing than others. African Asians seemed better prepared in terms of relevant skills, both technical/professional and business experience, although Indians seemed to exhibit an entrepreneurial flair in terms of being influenced by market opportunities. On the other hand, Pakistani entry into a particular line of business appeared to be less well-planned, with few reporting they had the appropriate technical or professional skills necessary to succeed in a particular line of business or having had past experience in a similar line of business.

Considering these differences between groups, both economic and cultural factors seem to be more favourable to the success of Indian business and least favourable for Pakistani. Indians more often seemed to enter self-employment for positive reasons, to take a market approach to business choice, to have better financial resources and to have family assistance as co-owners and workers. Pakistanis were more often driven into self-employment, seemed to lack access to capital and received less family help in running the business. On the positive side, however, family support was given for finance. African Asians fell between the two, having difficulties with finance, but possessing technical, professional and management skills to bring into play. The extent to which this picture is born out in the development and success of the business is the subject of the following two chapters.

Notes

1 Note that these dates may not reflect the South Asian pattern of entry into self-employment, as the sample is of South Asians who were still self-employed in 1994.

2 The questionnaire distinguished between self-employment as a full-time activity and as a part-time activity. Given the small numbers who had been self-employed part-time, this distinction is not made in the remainder of the book: all discussion about movement into self-employment refers to movement into self-employment as a full-time activity.

3 Equivalent to 18 per cent of the whole sample.

4 In order to ensure unpaid family assistance was reported, respondents were asked about those who 'worked or helped, in your business, paid or unpaid'. Thus the data cover both full-time employees and people who occasionally helped, unpaid, in the business.

Chapter 5

BUSINESS DEVELOPMENT

Research on ethnic minority businesses, like earlier small business research in general, has concentrated on business start-up and the pattern of existing business. The development of the business has received less attention. An issue we wished to explore was whether the pattern of self-employment among South Asians resulted from differences in business development and the factors which influenced business development. This chapter concentrates on these issues examining the change which took place from the date of entering self-employment full-time to the present.

Entrepreneurial change takes place at the level of the business and at the level of the entrepreneur. At the business level, a business may grow or decline and the range of products may change; at the level of the entrepreneur, new business may be acquired or started, existing businesses may be sold. At the extreme, a business may go bankrupt or an individual may move out of self-employment. Key indicators of these aspects of change include number of businesses owned, the products and services provided, turnover and employment size. The change in these indicators since start-up, together with more qualitative indicators (hours worked and the types of employees), are described below. The chapter then discusses factors which may have influenced change.

CHANGE IN THE SHAPE AND NATURE OF BUSINESS

Business change and development through starting, closing, buying or selling businesses was rare. Most respondents had started in self-employment with a single business and continued in self-employment with that business only (Table 5.1).

Table 5.1   Change in businesses owned, by ethnic group

				column percentages
	Indian	African Asian	Pakistani	All South Asians
Own original business only	77	89	84	81
Own original and other business(es)	2	3	10	5
Own other business(es) only	15	3	3	9
No longer self-employed	6	6	3	6
Unweighted base	*52*	*35*	*31*	*125*

Eighty-six per cent of the self-employed still owned their original business, although 5 per cent now owned an additional business (or businesses). Of the remainder, 6 per cent had ceased being self-employed in the year preceding the survey and 9 per cent owned a different business.[1] The degree of change was small overall. However, there appeared to be a greater tendency for Indians to change businesses and for African Asians to make no change at all.

The major reasons why these South Asian entrepreneurs no longer owned their original businesses were because they had sold their business (12 out of 18); because they had given the business to someone else (3 out of 18); and because they had decided to close it down (3 out of 18). None of the sample said they had lost ownership of the business because they had gone bankrupt.

When our sample of South Asian self-employed started in business full-time, only 1 per cent owned more than one business. By the time of the survey, that figure had grown to 8 per cent, with 6 per cent owning two businesses and 2 per cent owning three (Table 5.2). There was no difference in multiple business holding across ethnic groups. The main reasons given for the increase in the number of businesses owned were a desire to increase income and a desire to have a spread of businesses.

Table 5.2   The number of businesses owned currently, by ethnic group

column percentages

	Indian	African Asian	Pakistani	All South Asians
None (no longer self-employed)	4	6	3	5
One	88	89	90	88
Two	6	6	3	6
Three	2	0	3	2
Unweighted base	*51*	*36*	*31*	*124*

The other aspect of change in the nature of business is change within the business in the products and services sold. This was examined for the original business only. Here, again, change was uncommon. Of the high proportion who continued to own their original business only 16 per cent had made any substantial change in products or services (Table 5.3). There was no difference by ethnic group.

Table 5.3   Change in products and services of initial business

column percentages

	Indian	African Asians	Pakistani	All South Asians
Changed products/services	15	15	16	16
*Unweighted base**	*41*	*33*	*31*	*110*

* Base is those who still own their original business.

Thus, in terms of the shape and nature of business, the picture was one of stability. Most of the self-employed started a business, continued to run that same business without substantially changing its products, and did not add further businesses to their portfolio. Indians seemed most likely to make changes, through moving from their original business to another, whilst African Asians seemed least likely to make any change.

CHANGE IN TURNOVER AND CURRENT INCOME

Almost half the self-employed had seen growth, in terms of turnover, from when they started in business: 47 per cent said their turnover had increased, just over a fifth (22 per cent) said their turnover had decreased, whilst just under a quarter (23 per cent) said it had stayed the same (Table 5.4). As most had started their business from scratch, an increase in turnover should be expected. Therefore more than a fifth (those whose turnover had decreased) might be considered to have been encountering problems.

Table 5.4   The change in business turnover since the owner first started in business

				column percentages
	Indian	African Asian	Pakistani	All South Asians
Increased	48	58	39	47
Stayed the same	27	11	27	23
Decreased	7	25	33	22
Can't say	17	6	0	9
*Unweighted base**	*52*	*36*	*33*	*128*

* This includes those six respondents who were no longer in business. They were asked to compare their turnover at the start of their business to when they went out of business.

Comparison across ethnic groups was hampered by the high proportion of Indians who would not describe the change in turnover.[2] Therefore the following should be treated with caution where comparison is made with Indians. There was some difference between the main ethnic groups with a greater proportion of African Asians (58 per cent) reporting they had increased their turnover than Indians (48 per cent) and Pakistanis (39 per cent). Conversely, a greater proportion of Pakistanis (33 per cent) said their turnover had actually decreased since they first set up in business compared to a quarter of African Asians (25 per cent) and only 7 per cent of Indians. Thus, African Asians exhibited a bipolar distribution, with more doing well, but also a relatively high proportion doing badly. Pakistanis were least likely to do well, whilst Indians rarely did badly.

On this occasion we did not ask monetary questions because of the high rate of refusal to such questions in the Fourth Survey. It is, however, just worth mentioning the answers we received from the self-employed in the Fourth Survey to the earnings/profits question. These are presented in Table 5.5, from which it can be seen that about two-thirds of all groups except the Indians were willing to state or estimate their pre-tax profits; only about 40 per cent of Indians were prepared to do so. The non-respondents were proportionally spread by gender and by business size except that refusal was more common among those with employees, the more so the larger the number of employees. Hence, the analysis probably understates the earnings, especially of South Asians. South Asians were incidentally more willing to give an answer if an Asian language was used in the interview.

The Fourth Survey, which consisted of a broad spectrum of ethnic groups, found considerable diversity in the earnings of the self-employed, with a fifth earning less than £115 and about 15 per cent earning more than £500 in 1994 (Table 5.5). There was in fact relatively little difference between whites and ethnic minorities taken together, except that ethnic minorities were half as likely again as whites to be earning more than £500 per week. There were, however, considerable differences between groups on the basis of the bands in which respondents said their earnings fell. About a quarter of whites and African Asians said they were earning more than £385 per week, compared with a third of

Indians, Chinese and, Caribbeans; on the other hand, only an eighth of Pakistanis said they were earning more (the Bangladeshi sample was too small for analysis but is shown separately). Indeed, nearly two-thirds of the Pakistanis stated earnings below £193, while two-fifths of whites and Chinese, a third of Indians and African Asians, and a quarter of the Caribbeans did so. The mean earnings for Indians, Chinese and Caribbeans were over a fifth higher than those of whites, while for Pakistanis they were a fifth lower than for whites. Also worthy of note is that when comparison was made with the earnings of employees in the Fourth Survey, it was found that while white employees earned more than their self-employed counterparts, the reverse was true of ethnic minorities except African Asian (Modood et al, 1997).

Table 5.5   Weekly earnings from self-employment, by ethnic group

column percentages

	All whites	Carib- bean	Indian Asian	African	Paki- stani	Chinese	All ethnic minorities
			Ethnic group				
Less than £115	19	13	19	18	29	16	19
£116 - 192	21	12	12	15	34	23	19
£193 - 289	21	21	19	23	9	29	20
£290 - 385	16	20	14	17	14	0	14
£386 - 500	10	18	11	7	8	3	9
More than £500	13	16	24	19	5	29	19
Mean	**£288**	**£347**	**£364**	**£307**	**£226**	**£354**	**£319**
Weighted count	*156*	*44*	*56*	*62*	*48*	*48*	*265*
Unweighted count	*142*	*32*	*48*	*49*	*53*	*23*	*218*
Refusal/Can't say	31	31	61	41	34	31	43

On this occasion, in order to avoid refusals and not jeopardise the quality of the interview we did not ask for a detailed level of income. Instead, respondents were asked to rate their income on a scale from very high to very low. While this did not give information about the level, it did have the benefit of suggesting satisfaction with income. Over two-thirds felt that their income was at a medium level (Table 5.6). Seventeen per cent felt it was low and 7 per cent that it was high. While Indians and African-Asians exhibited similar patterns, with almost all considering their income was medium or high, nearly half of Pakistanis (46 per cent) felt their income was low.

Table 5.6   Income from the business

			percentage of each ethnic group	
	Indian	African Asian	Pakistani	All South Asians
Respondent considers their income to be:				
Very high	0	3	3	2
High	9	6	0	5
Medium	77	83	49	70
Low	4	6	30	13
Very low	0	0	15	4
Won't say	9	3	3	5
Unweighted base	*53*	*36*	*33*	*128*

CHANGE IN EMPLOYMENT

A major issue surrounding the role of self-employment among ethnic minorities is the extent to which it provides not only a vehicle for the economic enhancement of the individual entrepreneur, but employment opportunities for others.

At the time of start-up, the majority of the self-employed had at least one person helping them in the business (see Chapter 4). However, the number of people assisting was rarely more than four. At the time of the survey, a similar proportion worked entirely on their own (38 per cent, compared with 40 per cent on start-up) (Tables 4.11 and 5.7). However, for those with assistance, the number of employees or other helpers had grown. For example, at start-up, 17 per cent had had only one other person working in the business and 14 per cent had had five or more. At the time of the survey, the proportion with only one other in the business had fallen to 10 per cent, whilst the proportion with five or more others in the business had grown to 25 per cent.

Table 5.7   The number of people employed or helping in the business at the time of survey, by ethnic group

column percentages

	Indian	African Asian	Pakistani	All South Asians
None	32	50	39	38
One	10	15	6	10
Two	14	6	10	10
Three – Four	16	12	23	17
Five – Nine	14	6	10	13
Ten or more	14	12	13	12
Unweighted base	*50*	*34*	*31*	*121*

The total number of people employed (paid or unpaid) by these businesses had grown from 362 at start-up to 576 at the time of the survey, with the average, across all businesses, growing from three people (other than the owner) to five working in the business. Among those that had any employees (paid or unpaid) the average had grown from five to eight. Both at business start-up and at the time of the survey, these figures were skewed by a small number of businesses employing very large numbers of people. For example, at the time of the survey, 12 businesses employed 273 people between them, an average of almost 23 employees per firm.

Growth had taken place mainly in Indian and Pakistani businesses, with both these groups showing an increase in employment (paid or unpaid), particularly in the higher employment bands (Tables 4.11 and 5.7). Expansion had resulted in particularly large increases in businesses employing (paid or unpaid) five or more people, growing, for Indians, from 12 per cent on start-up to 28 per cent and, for Pakistanis, from 6 per cent on start-up to 23 per cent. It is worth noting that this marks a deviation in our sample from the Fourth Survey. In the latter, while about 15 per cent of African Asians and Indian businesses had five or more paid employees, only 5 per cent of Pakistanis did (Modood et al, 1997). The difference may be accounted for by the number of unpaid employees, though the difference between the proportion of businesses that used unpaid family help (about one in five) was not significant. It may be, however, that the Pakistani businesses that used unpaid help used more unpaid help per business – which would be consistent with the larger family size among the Pakistanis.

Comparing patterns of employment at start-up and at the time of the survey hides some of the complexity of change, as some businesses grew while others declined. Turning to the change experienced by each entrepreneur, we find that a high proportion of Pakistani businesses (39 per cent) had grown, African Asian businesses were most stable in terms of size, whereas Indian businesses showed more flux, with relatively high proportions growing or declining in size (Table 5.8).

Table 5.8   The change in the number of people working in the business from when it first started to the present

				column percentages
	Indian	African Asian	Pakistani	All South Asians
Now has more workers	24	18	38	25
Same number of workers	66	79	56	68
Now has fewer workers	10	3	6	7
Unweighted base	*50*	*34*	*32*	*122*

These changes seemed to be altering the patterns of employment across ethnic groups. At start-up, Indian businesses were more likely to have had employees (paid or unpaid) and especially to have had family workers, and, conversely, Indians had been least likely to have worked alone. Business development resulted in the proportion of Indian businesses with employees, especially with non-family workers, increasing (Table 5.9). The proportion of Pakistani businesses with employees (paid and unpaid) expanded even more rapidly, but with the concentration on family workers. African Asians remained the only group in which owners were at least equally likely to work alone as to have employees.

Table 5.9   Family and non-family employed or helping in the business at
the time of survey, by ethnic group

column percentages

	Indian	African Asian	Pakistani	All South Asians
No employees	32	50	39	38
Family only	18	26	26	21
Non-family only	12	6	6	12
Both	38	18	29	28
Some family	56	44	55	50
Some non-family	50	24	35	40
Unweighted base	50	34	31	121

Table 5.10   Numbers employed by the business today, by ethnic group

number of workers

	Indian	African Asian	Pakistani	All South Asians
Family worker	59	46	40	145
Non-family worker	231	79	115	454
Number of businesses with workers	34	17	19	75

Business development had not only changed the number of people working in the business. As might be expected, with growth, the degree to which owners relied on family workers had declined. Whilst a similar proportion of businesses (50 per cent compared with 46 per cent at start-up) continued to employ (paid or unpaid) relatives, the number employing others had grown (from 29 per cent to 40 per cent) (Tables 4.12 and 5.9). As Table 5.10 shows, approximately a quarter were family workers whilst the remainder were non-family workers. This confirms the developing similarity between Pakistani and Indian businesses. It also shows that African Asian businesses were not only remaining smaller, but had a greater tendency to remain family businesses, not employing other people (though in the Fourth

Survey African Asian businesses had more employees than Pakistani businesses and had the smallest proportion of family members among partners and paid employees).

Thus most businesses remained small family-run enterprises, although a small but significant minority of businesses did expand, of which some became large employers of labour. Whilst these businesses have increased employment, particularly providing jobs outside the family, when considering the degree to which South Asian entrepreneurs provide a source of jobs, it should be remembered that many of these businesses have been in operation for more than ten years and that the sample does not include those who failed in business other than in the last year. Thus the job creation potential of South Asian entrepreneurs is generally small, though the twelve largest businesses (nearly 10 per cent of the sample) employed 273 people.

Not surprisingly, the most common reason for increasing employment (paid or unpaid) was due to business expansion. Business expansion was more likely to lead to employment expansion for Pakistanis than for other groups (28 per cent, compared with 18 per cent of Indians and 15 per cent of African Asians). As fewer Pakistani businesses saw growth in turnover (39 per cent compared with 48 per cent of Indians and 58 per cent of African Asians), this shows a much higher tendency for Pakistanis to expand employment with growth. It was not possible to identify the reasons for this, except that as noted above it may denote the fact that Pakistanis have larger families and so more family individuals participate per business.

A number of reasons were given for reduction in the number of employees (paid or unpaid) in the business. Each was mentioned by three respondents or fewer. Not surprisingly, the most common were connected with business decline; never having had enough work for the number of employees was another reason. Not all reasons for decline were negative and change in production techniques had resulted in needing fewer workers. However, none mentioned change in technology having the same effect.

CHANGES IN HOURS WORKED

The number of hours worked in the business is one indicator of the quality of life derived from the business. On starting in business, new owners might be expected to work long hours: partly because of the desire and need to get the business off the ground and partly because of the possible lack of experience of running a business. However, this might continue (or increase) if the business runs into problems or expands, although, conversely, decreased hours might result from lack of work or from better control of the business. It was thought unrealistic to ask respondents to recall the number of hours they had worked on start-up, often many years previously. Instead, respondents estimated their current average hours and judged whether these had increased or decreased since start-up.

Table 5.11   **Current hours of work**

	Indian	African Asian	Pakistani	All South Asians
			percentage of each ethnic group	
Under 30	4	3	6	4
30 to under 40	0	6	13	6
40 to under 50	22	26	28	25
50 to under 60	41	41	34	37
60 to under 70	8	0	0	3
70 to under 80	14	21	9	17
80 or more	10	3	9	7
Unweighted base	*49*	*34*	*32*	*121*

Hours tended to be long. More than one quarter of the self-employed worked 60 hours or more per week on average and a third worked 50 to 60 hours (Table 5.11). Less than one third worked within the normal range for employees (30 to under 50 hours). Four per cent worked under 30 hours, the commonly used definition for part-time work. Differences across ethnic groups were not extensive. Indians, however, had a greater tendency to work longer hours (32 per cent worked 60 hours or more and only 4 per cent worked less than 40 hours, whereas Pakistanis tended to work somewhat shorter hours (18 per cent worked 60 hours or more, while 19 per cent worked under 40 hours).

Over half (57 per cent) of the self-employed sample continued to work the same number of hours as when they first started (Table 5.12). More had managed to reduce their hours (27 per cent) than had increased their hours (16 per cent). There was some difference across the three main ethnic groups. Indians tended to exhibit more stability in hours, with almost three-quarters (72 per cent) working the same number of hours as when they first started, compared to just under half of African Asians (47 per cent) and Pakistanis (47 per cent). A third of African Asians (32 per cent) and Pakistanis (34 per cent) said they worked shorter hours now than when they first started up in business compared to one fifth of Indian business owners (18 per cent). Interestingly, almost twice as many African Asians (21 per cent) and Pakistanis (19 per cent) reported working longer hours than Indians (10 per cent).

Table 5.12 The change in the number of hours worked by the owner from first starting in business to the present, by ethnic group

				column percentages
	Indian	African Asian	Pakistani	All South Asians
Now works longer hours	10	21	19	16
Works the same number of hours	72	47	47	57
Now works shorter hours	18	32	34	27
Unweighted base	*50*	*34*	*32*	*121*

The reasons for change in the number of hours worked displayed different responses to changing circumstances and the degree to which different owners had increased their control over the business. Business expansion was the most common reason for increasing hours (Table 5.13). However, this was matched by those increasing hours in order to stay in business, while business contraction had led to six owners decreasing their hours (Table 5.14). Shorter hours were most often worked in response to the stress caused by long hours or because the owner had improved control over the business (they were better organised, delegated more or had recruited staff). Some had also decreased their hours because of loss of interest or preference for other activities, while only two said they worked longer hours because they enjoyed it.

Table 5.13   The reasons for working longer hours today

				absolute number
	Indian	African Asian	Pakistani	All South Asians
Business expanded	3	4	3	12
To stay in business	3	4	3	10
Can't get good staff	0	0	2	2
I enjoy it	1	1	0	2
Other	2	3	1	6
Unweighted base	5	7	6	19

Table 5.14   The reasons for working shorter hours today

				column percentages
	Indian	African Asian	Pakistani	All South Asians
Longer hours were too stressful	1	4	4	11
Better organised	2	5	2	9
Delegate more	0	1	1	2
Recruited staff	1	0	2	3
Business contracted	1	3	2	6
Less interested	1	0	0	1
Other activities more important	1	0	2	3
Other	4	4	5	13
Unweighted base	9	11	11	33

FACTORS AFFECTING BUSINESS DEVELOPMENT

The business changes described above resulted from a range of influences. The owner's business skills and attitudes will have affected business development, as will external factors outside the owner's control (although business skills and attitudes will have determined the response to external change). This section discusses a number of factors affecting business development, concentrating on issues related to attitudes and approaches to business.

ORIGINAL INTENTIONS FOR THE BUSINESS

Right from the start, individuals had different approaches to their business: about whether they wished to expand and why. Just over half had wanted to expand their business (54 per cent) compared to a third (34 per cent) who had wished it to the stay the same size. None had sought contraction, although 12 per cent had been unsure about whether they wished to expand or not (Table 5.15). There was no difference by ethnic group.

Table 5.15   Plans and intentions for the business at start-up, by ethnic group

column percentages

	Indian	African Asian	Pakistani	All South Asians
Expand	52	58	52	54
Stay the same size	33	31	39	34
Contract	0	0	0	0
Don't know	15	11	9	12
Unweighted base	*52*	*36*	*33*	*128*

The most common reasons affecting business intentions were money (45 per cent wanted to expand in order to make more money), avoidance of stress (23 per cent did not want to expand because they felt it would cause too much stress), and social status (12 per cent wanted to expand for this reason) (Tables 5.16 and 5.17). Twelve per cent also wanted to expand because it enabled them to keep up with demand. Other reasons, given by a small proportion wanting to expand, included preparation for retirement and to provide a large business for the children.

Table 5.16   The reasons why the self-employed, on becoming self-employed, wanted their business to expand, by ethnic group

column percentages

	Indian	African Asian	Pakistani	All South Asians
To make more money	39	50	40	45
To improve social status	9	13	9	12
To keep up with demand for products/services	21	8	3	12
To provide basis for retirement	5	6	6	7
Wanted large business for children	3	3	6	5
Large businesses are less risky	3	3	3	3
Other	0	8	9	5
Unweighted base	52	36	33	128

There were significant differences between ethnic groups. African Asians were more likely to be motivated to want to expand by the desire to make more money (50 per cent compared with 40 per cent of Pakistanis and 39 per cent of Indians). This suggests that, although a similar proportion of each group had rated money as important, in fact, for African Asians this assumed more importance in relation to the business. Indians were more likely to be prompted to expand due to market demand (21 per cent, compared with 8 per cent of African Asians and 3 per cent of Pakistanis). The desire to avoid stress was most likely to discourage Pakistanis from wanting to expand (30 per cent) and least likely to discourage Indians (19 per cent).

Table 5.17 The reasons why the self-employed, on becoming self-employed, did not want their business to expand, by ethnic group

column percentages

	Indian	African Asian	Pakistani	All South Asians
Would cause too much stress	19	22	30	23
Business would take up too much time	4	11	6	6
Didn't need any more money	4	5	6	5
Other	9	3	12	8
Unweighted base	*52*	*36*	*33*	*128*

MARKETS AND SKILLS

Respondents were asked why their turnover had increased or declined. Although it was not possible to distinguish clearly between external market factors and the self-employed's activities shaping their place in the market, the responses suggested some interesting differences across ethnic groups.

Business skills were the most common factor attributed to affecting growth in turnover. Almost half of the whole sample said that their turnover growth was (at least in part) due to building up custom and a further 19 per cent mentioned good marketing (Table 5.18). Furthermore, 17 per cent of businesses had grown due to expansion into new products or services. Factors which were more closely related to markets were important for many: increased demand was cited by 29 per cent as a factor in increasing turnover and a reduction in competition was cited by 5 per cent. At the same time, market factors were most often attributed as responsible for a fall in turnover (greater competition, 13 per cent, and fall in demand, 6 per cent) (Table 5.19).

Table 5.18   The reasons turnover increased, by ethnic group

column percentages

	Indian	African Asian	Pakistani	All South Asians
Built up custom	35	39	21	46
Good marketing	13	11	12	19
Expanded into new products/services	13	14	6	17
Price increase	6	60	3	7
Increased demand for products	31	14	12	29
Less competition	8	0	0	5
Other	13	6	12	15
Unweighted base	52	36	33	128

Table 5.19   The reasons turnover decreased, by ethnic group

column percentages

	Indian	African Asian	Pakistani	All South Asians
Lost customers	0	3	15	5
Price decrease	0	0	3	1
Fall in demand for the product	4	3	15	6
Change in fashion	0	0	3	1
Greater competition	6	14	18	13
Other	2	11	12	7
Unweighted base	52	36	33	128

Indians seemed to be best positioned in terms of markets: 31 per cent attributed increase in turnover to increased demand for products, compared with 14 per cent of African Asians and 12 per cent of Pakistanis, and only Indians saw a decrease in competition as increasing turnover. At the same time, fewer Indians thought their turnover had decreased due to market factors (fall in demand, greater competition, change in fashion). Both African

Asians and Indians were equally likely to see growth in turnover resulting from business skills, with 35 per cent of Indians and 39 per cent of African Asians attributing growth to building up custom. Pakistanis seemed to suffer on both the market and business skills fronts: fewer (compared with Indians) saw growth due to market factors and more (than both Indians and African Asians) saw decline; and fewer (than either Indians or African Asians) saw growth due to business skills (particularly in building up custom).

This pattern would follow from the background to self-employment exhibited by the three groups (see Chapters 2 and 4). Pakistanis, the group who seemed most often to be escaping into self-employment, rather than choosing it for positive reasons, had least often chosen the business line for business reasons. They were also the least educated and had rarely picked up business skills from their previous employment. Conversely, it might be expected that the higher educational levels of the Indians and African Asians assisted them in developing business skills. Moreover, more African Asians had developed such skills through their previous employment. Finally, Indians seemed to have been most guided by business reasons (rather than job-specific skills) over choice of business.

THE BUSINESS AS A VEHICLE FOR FAMILY EMPLOYMENT

Over time, businesses increased employment and shifted the balance between family and non-family workers. As the discussion above showed, developments differed across ethnic groups. The study explored the role of different attitudes towards the family in influencing the decision on whom to employ.

Owners who had family members working in the business were asked the reasons for this. Business reasons were common: family members were better workers (74 per cent) and the business could not afford other employees (47 per cent). (This latter reason suggests that many businesses were highly precarious.) However, non-business reasons were also very common, with many owners influenced in their decisions by desire for family solidarity and to provide general assistance to their family members. Sixty-three per cent employed (paid or unpaid) family members in the business because they saw this as keeping the family together (Table 5.20). Around a fifth to a quarter gave other reasons which related to showing responsibility to the family (to keep the family in work, the lack of decent jobs, the alternative of unemployment). Employment decisions made on these grounds may result in less appropriate workers (although, given the low skill-level of most of the jobs, this may not be a problem) and may therefore inhibit business survival and development. On the other hand, such decisions are more likely to enhance the economic well-being of the family unit.

Table 5.20   Reasons for family working in the business

column percentages

	Indian	African Asian	Pakistani	All South Asians
Better workers	80	87	53	74
Can't afford employees	40	47	60	47
Keeps family together	80	73	26	63
Responsibility to keep family in work	28	13	20	21
No other decent jobs	28	20	34	27
Would be unemployed otherwise	20	7	40	21
Prefer to work in same religious group	4	13	13	10
Prefer to work in same ethnic group	8	7	7	8
Family does not need to work for money	4	7	7	5
*Unweighted base**	*25*	*15*	*15*	*55*

* Base is those who had family workers.
Respondents were asked to give up to three reasons.

The numbers involved make comment on the differences across groups somewhat speculative. However, Pakistanis seemed to be more often influenced by the relative cost of family and non-family workers. Family solidarity, in terms of keeping the family together, was less of a concern of Pakistanis than Indians or African Asians, but avoiding their unemployment was more of a concern. While these differences could suggest Pakistanis placed less emphasis on the business as a vehicle for family solidarity, together with the other evidence a more likely explanation seems to be a greater precariousness of Pakistani businesses combined with poor employment prospects, resulting in an emphasis on economic necessity.

RELIGION

Religion has already been mentioned as an influence on the nature of the business entered and on access to capital. These start-up factors may have a continuing influence on the business, but religion may have other effects on development. In particular, they may have affected the goods and services sold and the ability to raise finance for expansion. This section discusses goods and services, and finance is discussed in the following section.

Religion affected the goods and services which could be provided by one quarter of the self-employed (Table 5.21). This affected two-thirds of Pakistanis. Fewer African Asians, one quarter, were affected, and hardly any Indians. However, whilst religion might be reported as affecting the provision of certain goods and services, this is only important where those goods and services might otherwise have actually been considered. This was explored in relation to alcohol and meat/meat products.

Table 5.21   **Religion and business**

	Indian	African Asian	Pakistani	All South Asians
			percentage of each ethnic group	
Religion influences the goods and services which can be provided	2	24	66	27
Religion has a view on handling alcohol	8	32	97	41
Alcohol is relevant to the business	0	6	31	13
Does handle alcohol	0	3	6	6
Not considered, due to religion	0	0	25	7
Not considered (not due to religion)	0	3	0	1
Religion has a view on the handling of meat/ meat products	16	41	87	44
Handling of meat/ meat products relevant to business	6	12	38	20
Does handle meat/ meat products	6	12	31	18
Not considered, due to religion	0	0	6	2
Not considered (not due to religion)	0	0	0	0
*Unweighted base**	*51*	*34*	*32*	*123*

* Base varied slightly over questions: base is those self-employed at the time of the survey.

As we saw in Chapter 3, two-fifths of the self-employed reported that their religion had a view on the handling of alcohol. However, only 13 per cent reported that handling alcohol was relevant to their business. Of these about half did handle alcohol, despite their religion, and half did not because of their religion. Thus, only a small proportion, 7 per cent, reported religious views on alcohol as putting any constraint on their business. However, there were major differences by ethnic group. One quarter of all Pakistani businesses reported that the handling of alcohol was relevant to their business but that due to their religion they did not consider handling it. Alcohol was not a constraint for either Indians or African Asians. While these figures should not be taken to mean that all these businesses would have handled alcohol, but for the religious views of the owners, it does, however, suggest that Pakistani businesses are constrained and that others are not.

Although a similar proportion of the self-employed held religious views on the handling of meat/meat products (44 per cent), the effect on business was slight, as nearly all those for whom it was relevant handled meat/meat products regardless of their religious views.

ACCESS TO CAPITAL

The role of religion, family, friends and institutions in relation to start-up funding was discussed in Chapter 4, where it was shown that personal savings, the bank, family and friends were the most common sources of finance. The pattern of finance for expansion was somewhat different. Firstly, businesses tended to use a single source, rather than multiple sources (Table 5.22). Savings remained the most common source, used by 48 per cent of those who expanded (compared with 68 per cent at start-up). Once in business, of course, retained profits became a source of finance for expansion and were used by 39 per cent of those who expanded. Borrowing from the bank declined in usage (from 42 per cent on start-up to 27 per cent for expansion) but was still an important source, and finance from family and friends became unimportant.

At start-up, each ethnic group appeared to have different access to each source of finance and this appeared to be related to religion, family networks and ability to meet institutional demands (Chapter 4). Unfortunately, the numbers involved in business expansion make comparison across ethnic groups impossible.

Table 5.22 Sources of finance for business expansion, by ethnic group

column percentages

	Indian	African Asian	Pakistani	All South Asians
Savings	64	24	56	48
Retained profits from the business	44	29	56	39
Bank	32	29	22	27
Loans from friends	12	0	11	7
Loans from family	4	0	22	5
Other	8	33	11	18
Unweighted base	*25*	*21*	*9*	*56*

SUMMARY AND CONCLUSION

Thus, in terms of the shape and nature of business, the picture was one of stability. Most of the self-employed started a business, continued to run that same business without substantially changing its products, and did not add further businesses to their portfolio.

However, organisational stability did not seem to lead to financial security. About one half had seen their turnover increase, but for others stability seemed linked with stagnation or decline. At the same time, most continued to work very long hours. Rather fewer grew in terms of number of workers in the business and most remained small individual or family businesses. Six per cent of the self-employed had come to own two businesses, and 2 per cent owned three.

Patterns of business development across ethnic groups differed. Indians were most likely to make changes in the structure of the business and rarely did badly in terms of turnover.[3] Growth resulted in development away from family businesses to businesses employing others. On the other hand, change and success did not appear cost-free, with Indians tending to work the longest hours. African Asian businesses were most stable, in terms of organisational structure and employment (tending to remain single person businesses), but, in terms of turnover, showed a bipolar distribution, with a high proportion doing well and a high proportion doing badly. In terms of organisational change, Pakistani businesses lay between the two, but they were least likely to do well. Yet, despite poorer turnover performance, more Pakistani businesses showed employment (paid or unpaid) growth. This was mainly through employing more family and resulted in the employment structure of Indian and Pakistani businesses becoming more similar. Though findings from the Fourth Survey suggest that the businesses with the most employees are likely to be African Asian and Indian rather than Pakistani, it confirms that self-employment produces much better financial rewards for African Asians and Indians than for Pakistanis.

Across ethnic groups, development seemed to follow in the way that might be expected from the resources and approaches available at start-up. Indians, who had exhibited a business approach to setting up, had good access to finance and seemed to enter business for positive reasons, rarely did badly. At the same time, they were the group most likely to make organisational changes, through moving from their original business to another. The reasons they gave for successful growth suggested that they were, indeed, best positioned in terms of markets and that they were applying business skills in order to develop.

Pakistanis, who seemed to have had the least resources (financial and skill) and who seemed to have been pushed into self-employment, were least likely to see their turnover grow and many experienced decline. It appeared as if lack of business skills, possibly combined with wrong initial choice of business (in a declining or highly competitive market) resulted in decline. Recognition of a lack of business skills may have been indicated by the relatively high proportion of Pakistanis who at the outset did not wish to expand and who gave the reason as avoidance of stress, perhaps thus recognising the difficulties of running a larger business. (Alternatively, of course, this might also indicate a lesser ability or willingness to cope with stress.) One aspect of religion may have exerted a brake on the development of Pakistani businesses, in that many (where it would have been relevant) did not handle alcohol for religious reasons. However, more Pakistani businesses grew in terms of employment (although not to the same extent as Indian businesses). As growth was most commonly linked to business expansion, there could be a number of reasons for this: the nature of the business may have necessitated employment growth with business growth (that is lack of employment economies of scale); the proportionate size of business growth may have been greater (and therefore impossible to cover without more employees); or other groups may have used their greater business skills to reorganise with business growth, reducing the need for more workers. On the other hand, as growth meant primarily bringing in family workers and avoiding their unemployment, growth may have also been due either to bringing in available labour at the margins or to the business being used to create work (rather than the business requiring more employees).

The greater diversity of the African Asian self-employed (in terms of education, religion and type of business) helps explain their bipolar experience in terms of turnover growth (a high proportion doing well and a high proportion doing badly) and changes in hours. For those that grew, business skills seemed important. However, as many grew due to price increases, markets may also have played a role.[4] For many, this may have been a fortuitous initial choice, as professional and technical skills had tended to guide the line of business entered. The skill-based choice of business may also explain the lack of organisational change and employment growth, as many of the businesses were of the type in which lone self-employment is common. This may have been reinforced by the desire to avoid risk, identified in Chapter 3.

This discussion highlights the development of the business being largely influenced by economic factors and by the factors surrounding initial entry into business. However, the role of culture should not be overlooked. Some cultural influences have been identified and culture will have influenced business development via its affect on start-up. Moreover, some of the ways in which culture may have had an affect (such as access to capital) could not be examined due to smallness of numbers. The family was seen as a source of good labour and the employment of family members in the business was influenced by the desire to keep the family together.

Finally, this chapter has discussed the role of self-employment as providing employment generally. Although some businesses expanded their employment substantially, most businesses remained small individual or family-run enterprises. With expansion, the number of employees outside the family grew in particular. However, given the period of operation of many of these businesses (and the exclusion of those which had failed prior to the initial survey), the amount of job creation was small, except in the largest 10 per cent of the business.

Notes

1   Of course the 6 per cent leaving self-employment does not represent the extent of turnover of self-employed South Asians, as there will be many who entered and went out of business at an earlier stage and so could not form part of the survey sample.

2   Questions on the size of turnover had been avoided because of an expectation of a reluctance to give such information. The difficulty over comparisons suggests that the expectation of sensitivity was well-founded.

3   A high proportion, 17 per cent, of Indians did not describe the change in turnover. Therefore conclusions about Indian businesses must be treated with caution.

4   As respondents were not asked whether they were following or making price increases, the influence of markets and of business skills could not be disentangled.

Chapter 6

THE BENEFITS OF SELF-EMPLOYMENT

The previous chapters have looked at the factors affecting the pattern of self-employment among South Asians in Britain. This has suggested differences among the three main groups, stemming from religion, community, education and economic circumstances. Self-employment has appeared to be taken as a way out from racism and poor employment prospects for some, particularly Pakistanis, but more often as a positive choice for Indians and African-Asians. Reflecting this, self-employed Indians and African-Asians have tended to have better skills and support for self-employment compared with Pakistanis. This would lead one to expect differences in attachment to the business, satisfaction and success across groups, and, as shown in the previous chapter, this seems to have been the case in terms of outcomes such as turnover.

This chapter focuses on whether self-employment offered a positive experience for respondents or whether it was the 'economic dead-end' described by the first major research on British Asian self-employment (Aldrich et al, 1981). It starts with respondents' own assessment of their success in business, comparing this with achievement of success in conventional business terms. However, self-employment may offer much more than conventional business benefits and the extent to which respondents experienced other benefits (and problems) are described: self-worth, family cohesion, interest, independence, demands on time and income. The chapter then discusses commitment to self-employment, using evidence on intentions to expand and to retire. Whether the business is regarded as good enough for their children and whether they wish their children to take over the business provides final evidence on how respondents see their business.

SUCCESS

Success in business can mean many different things. Conventional business measurements focus on turnover, profit and size. When entering self-employment, about half of the respondents in each ethnic group had aimed to expand their business. Chapter 5 has described the degree of success achieved in this aim.

- For almost half (49 per cent) turnover had increased, whilst 21 per cent had experienced a reduction. By ethnic group, African Asians showed a bipolar pattern, with the highest proportion of growth (62 per cent) but a high proportion declining (21 per cent); Indians were almost as successful at growing (50 per cent) with few declining (8 per cent); while Pakistanis tended to do relatively poorly with 41 per cent growing and 34 per cent contracting.

- In employment terms, one quarter had grown, whilst only 7 per cent had declined (although most had started with no employees). More Pakistani businesses grew and African Asian businesses were least likely to grow (38 per cent and 18 per cent respectively grew, whilst 24 per cent of Indian businesses grew). There was no difference in contraction across ethnic groups.

- The Fourth Survey suggested that the largest and the most financially rewarding businesses tended to be African Asian and Indian, though even Pakistani average earnings were higher among those in self-employment than as employees.

Against this pattern of growth and decline, a high proportion of respondents (84 per cent) felt they had been successful in business, although only a small proportion (13 per cent) felt they had been very successful (Table 6.1). Not surprisingly, given the differences in growth of turnover, more Indians and African Asians felt they had been successful in business than Pakistanis. However, across all ethnic groups, there was a tendency for respondents to consider themselves as having been successful even when turnover had declined.

Table 6.1   Self-assessment of success in business

	Indian	African Asian	Pakistani	All South Asians
			percentage of each ethnic group	
Very successful	13	17	9	13
Fairly successful	79	69	67	71
Not very successful	6	11	18	12
Not at all successful	0	3	3	2
Don't know	2	0	3	2
Unweighted base	*53*	*36*	*33*	*129*

An important aspect of both success in business and satisfaction with self-employment will be the income derived from the business. Indeed, 68 per cent of respondents gave increasing their income as a reason for setting up in business, with 83 per cent of African Asians, 72 per cent of Pakistanis and 52 per cent of Indians concerned in this respect. In Chapter 5 we saw that while nearly all Indians and African Asians considered their income to be medium or high, nearly half of Pakistanis felt their income was low (Table 5.6).

Given these feelings about income, it was not surprising that Pakistanis were more likely to report financial difficulties (38 per cent) (Table 6.2). The expected link between how high one rated one's income, how well one managed financially and money worries occurred for Indians and Pakistanis, but not for African Asians, who, despite almost all considering they had medium to high incomes, were as likely as Pakistanis to worry about money and almost as likely to have financial difficulties.

Table 6.2   Financial problems

	Indian	African Asian	Pakistani	All South Asians
			percentage of each ethnic group	
How well managing financially:				
Very well	6	6	9	6
Fairly well	79	69	48	68
Some difficulties/ deep problems*	9	22	36	21
Can't say/not answered	6	3	6	5
How often worrying about money:				
Almost all the time	4	25	15	13
Quite often	17	19	27	20
Occasionally	66	47	49	55
Never	11	8	6	10
Can't say/not answered	2	0	3	2
Unweighted base	*53*	*36*	*33*	*129*

* 6 per cent of Pakistanis and 14 per cent of Bangladeshis said they had deep problems, all the rest reported some difficulties.

This evidence of different views about money was also supported by the extent to which respondents saved. Overall, 41 per cent saved regularly, but only 27 per cent of African Asians did, compared with 42 per cent of Pakistanis and 55 per cent of Indians.

These differences cannot be explained in terms of differences in the importance of money across ethnic groups, as there was none. (About half of all respondents regarded money as very important in their life, with the remaining half regarding it as quite important, with no difference across ethnic groups.) If one accepts that people's views on the level of their income bear a relationship to the income they find acceptable to live on, it is tempting to attribute some differences to culture. As discussed in Chapter 3, Indians were more cautious than the other groups (risk averse and preferring old ideas to new). This, combined with considering their income medium to high, may have resulted in higher levels of saving and, consequently, fewer money worries than African Asians, despite the African Asians' similar views of their income level but their greater willingness to accept risk.

In any case, what is particularly clear from the self-assessment of success in business is that the sample did not equate the benefits of self-employment in purely financial terms, a finding that has also been made elsewhere (Srinivasan, 1995). We turn, therefore, to examine other ways in which individuals valued the potential and actual benefits of their self-employment.

IDENTITY AND SELF-WORTH

The business was very important in conferring on individuals feelings of worth and standing. Nearly all, 95 per cent, derived a feeling of self-worth from their business (Table 6.3). A greater proportion derived feelings of self-worth (95 per cent) and standing with their families (82 per cent) than with the wider community, whether their own ethnic or religious group (65 per cent) or British society at large (67 per cent).

Table 6.3   Identity and self-worth derived from the business

percentages

	Agree strongly	Agree a little	Neither	Disagree a little	Disagree strongly	Can't say
My work gives me standing in British Society	30	37	7	8	12	6
My work gives me standing in my ethnic/religious community	30	35	9	9	14	2
My work gives me standing with my family	46	36	7	5	5	2
My work gives me a feeling of self-worth	59	36	2	0	2	1

N = 129

Some differences were apparent across ethnic groups. More African Asians felt strongly that their business conferred self-worth (72 per cent) compared with Indians (59 per cent) and Pakistanis (39 per cent). There was some indication that fewer Pakistanis derived a feeling (whether strong or not) of standing in British society from their business (58 per cent) than did Indians (70 per cent) or African Asians (69 per cent). However, for all groups, only a quarter of each group had entered business with this aim (see Chapter 4). More African Asians felt strongly that their business gave them standing with the family (58 per cent) than Indians (37 per cent) and Pakistanis (42 per cent). This was an unfortunate pattern, given that achieving status within the family was a reason for becoming self-employed for many Pakistanis (53 per cent), African Asians (44 per cent) and Indians (25 per cent), suggesting that many will have not seen themselves as succeeding in this way. Thus it appears that African Asians were more successful in achieving self-worth and status. Given the greater desire to derive status through self-employment and the lack of achievement in this area, Pakistanis were particularly unsuccessful.

Obviously the nature of the business will affect both the extent to which individuals feel it confers self-worth and standing with others (professionals, for example, might believe they derive higher degrees of self-worth and standing than corner shop owners); some businesses may also confer differing degrees of self-worth and standing (for example, a mortuary worker might have a high degree of self-worth, but a feeling of low standing in society, whereas a bank manager might experience the opposite). However, differences in the types of businesses run by the three ethnic groups did not seem to explain fully the differences in self-worth and standing.

First, if African Asian businesses are objectively more worthwhile and impressive, followed by Indian businesses, with Pakistani businesses coming third in the league, this would explain the pattern, except for the fact that no more Indians than Pakistanis see their business as conferring status with their family. This suggests a cultural difference in perceptions of what achieves status within the family between these ethnic groups. This is supported by the smaller proportion of Indians who were motivated by the desire to increase their standing with their family through setting up in business. Alternatively, if there were no 'objective' difference in status of business across ethnic groups, then not only is there this difference between Indians and the other two groups in relation to the family, but in how each group derives satisfaction from their work.

Respondents also derived moral and religious benefits from their work. Three-quarters of respondents felt that their work made them a better person, while 41 per cent felt their work enabled them to perform their religious duties (Table 6.4). Distinct differences were apparent across ethnic groups. More Indians and African-Asians felt that their work made them a better person, around 80 per cent each, compared with only half of Pakistanis (54 per cent). 'Moral betterment' through their work was felt particularly by African Asians, with 50 per cent feeling strongly that their work made them a better person (compared with 21 per cent of Indians). Pakistanis saw the effect of work more in terms of enabling them to perform their religious duties. Two-thirds of Pakistanis felt this compared with one third of Indians and around one quarter of African Asians; 42 per cent of Pakistanis felt this strongly, compared with 17 per cent or fewer of the other two groups. Indeed, around one third of African Asians and Indians felt that their work did not enable them to perform their religious duties. The difference probably relates to Muslim religious obligations such as the requirement to pray five times a day. As some of these prayer times fall within the working day, it is likely that some Muslims feel that they are better able to discharge this obligation when they are their own boss than when an employee, for they may have an unsympathetic employer or an inflexible work pattern. Moreover, as we saw in the previous chapter, a quarter of the Pakistanis expressly chose not to handle alcohol, even though it was relevant to their business, an exercise of choice which they may not have had as employees. Given that nearly all Pakistanis said that religion was very important to how they lived, the 42 per cent who strongly felt that self-employment enabled them to perform their religious duties clearly have a reason to value self-employment.

Table 6.4   Moral and religious benefits

			percentage of each ethnic group
	Indian	African Asian	Pakistani	All South Asians

My work makes me a better person			
Agree strongly	21	50	24	32
Agree a little	60	31	30	43
Neither	8	17	24	15
Disagree a little	9	3	6	6
Disagree strongly	2	0	9	3
Can't say	0	0	6	2
My work enables me to perform my religious duties			
Agree strongly	11	17	42	21
Agree a little	23	8	24	20
Neither	26	33	15	25
Disagree a little	6	11	3	6
Disagree strongly	30	25	12	24
Can't say ˙	4	6	3	4
Unweighted base	*53*	*36*	*33*	*129*

FAMILY COHESION

We saw in the previous chapter that the family was seen by the self-employed as a source of good labour, and that the employment of family members in the business was influenced by the desire to deep the family together. Here we look at what extent the self-employed thought their business served the well-being of the family.

Table 6.5 shows that while opinion among the self-employed was split, a good proportion thought self-employment was advantageous in strengthening family life and cohesion. About half the sample (46 per cent) said their business provided jobs for the family and that it enabled family members to work together (47 per cent), while 35 per cent said their business allowed their wife to combine working with looking after the children.

Table 6.5   Business and family life

			column percentages
	Indian	African Asian	Pakistani	All South Asians

My business enables me to provide jobs for my family[*]			
Agree	50	41	45	46
Disagree	36	50	48	42

My business means that my family can work together			
Agree	53	38	47	47
Disagree	43	59	50	47

My business means that my wife can combine working with looking after the children[**]			
Agree	34	34	36	35
Disagree	55	66	57	57

Unweighted base[***]	50	34	31	121

[*]   Those who neither agreed nor disagreed are not shown in the table.

[**]   To women 'I' was substituted for 'my wife' in the question.

[***] Base varied between questions.

There was some variation by ethnic group: Indians (36 per cent) were less likely than African Asians (50 per cent) and Pakistanis (48 per cent) to disagree that self-employment enabled them to provide jobs for their family, whilst a greater proportion of Indians (53 per cent) and Pakistanis (47 per cent) than African Asians (38 per cent) said that the business allowed the family to work together.

While these views may have been expressing matters of fact (the family did work in the business, and therefore it worked together), Chapter 5 has already discussed the reasons for employing family workers and found that a high proportion were motivated by family cohesion or responsibility factors. The high proportion having such reasons for employing family workers lends support to Srinivasan's contention that the desire to maintain family cohesion is a key determinant of South Asian self-employment (Srinivasan, 1992 and 1995). It also suggests that many of the self-employed found success in self-employment through believing they were strengthening family cohesion by providing employment to family members.

OTHER INDICATORS OF SATISFACTION: INTEREST, INDEPENDENCE AND HOURS

A number of other benefits and indicators of satisfaction with the business were examined. Nearly all respondents gained interest from their work: 91 per cent were interested, with 63 per cent very interested. African Asians, particularly, found their work interesting (75 per cent strongly interested), while less than half of Pakistanis derived a great deal of interest (46 per cent). The difference might be due to the different types of businesses across ethnic groups and act in combination with the lower levels of education among Pakistanis.

Table 6.6   Interest and independence

			percentage of each ethnic group	
	Indian	African Asian	Pakistani	All South Asians
My work interests me				
Agree strongly	62	75	46	63
Agree a little	30	19	36	28
Neither	2	3	6	3
Disagree a little	2	0	0	1
Disagree strongly	4	3	12	5
My work enables me to be independent of others				
Agree strongly	53	72	67	63
Agree a little	38	14	30	29
Neither	6	8	0	5
Disagree a little	0	6	0	2
Disagree strongly	4	0	0	2
Can't say	0	0	3	1
Unweighted base	53	36	33	129

A desire for independence had played a role in setting up in business. For example, 47 per cent of Indians, 67 per cent of African Asians and 78 per cent of Pakistanis had given the desire to be their own boss as a reason for setting up in business (see Chapter 4). Ninety-two per cent had achieved some degree of independence, with 63 per cent gaining a lot of independence. Feelings of independence were highest among African Asians and Pakistanis. Compare with the initial desire for independence, this suggested that, although a high proportion of Pakistanis had achieved a feeling of independence, they were perhaps slightly less successful in this aim than others: more African Asians and Indians felt a high degree of independence than had sought it.

Table 6.7   Satisfaction with hours of work

			percentage of each ethnic group
	Indian	African Asian	Pakistani	All South Asians
Prefer to work current number of hours	22	24	22	23
Prefer to work fewer hours	68	50	50	57
Prefer to work more hours	2	12	19	10
Could not say	8	15	9	10
Unweighted base	*50*	*34*	*32*	*122*

In terms of hours of work, only a minority were satisfied with their hours of work with only 23 per cent wanting to work the hours they did. Most wanted to work fewer hours (57 per cent) and 10 per cent wanted to work more hours (Table 6.7). The hours worked varied across ethnic groups: there were relatively more Pakistanis and relatively fewer Indians among the small proportion working less than 40 hours per week and more Indians worked particularly long hours. This may explain the higher proportion of African Asians and Pakistanis wanting to work more hours and the higher proportion of Indians wanting to work fewer hours. The higher value placed on leisure among Indians than African Asians and Pakistanis may also contribute to this pattern: 59 per cent of Indians saw leisure as very important compared with 42 per cent of African Asians and 23 per cent of Pakistanis, while 8 per cent of Indians regarded leisure as not very important compared with 14 per cent of African Asians and 23 per cent of Pakistanis. However, these figures would lead to more African Asians wanting to reduce their hours. The difference could not be explained by differences in the age structure across ethnic groups leading to different priorities, as the self-employed in each group were of a similar age (Table 2.4).

COMMITMENT TO SELF-EMPLOYMENT

It is commonly claimed that South Asian immigrants have a predisposition towards self-employment. On the other hand, self-employment may be high among South Asians because it offers the best opportunities to immigrants, that is to say self-employment is a function of immigration and will decline among South Asians as second and subsequent generations develop. This issue was examined from a number of angles. Firstly, the emphasis placed on the business compared with other activities was explored. Secondly, future intentions were explored: expansion, retirement and the desire for children to take over the business.

Most respondents stated strong commitment to the business, stating they did the best for the business even when this interfered with the rest of their life (Table 6.8). Indians seemed to place slightly more emphasis on other activities than Pakistanis and African Asians. This would tally with Indians placing greater emphasis on the importance of leisure, but not of other activities, such as spending time with the family.

Plans for the future of the business are a good indicator of commitment and of satisfaction with the business. About one third of respondents (32 per cent) were planning to expand their business and the remainder wished to stay the same size. There was no significant difference between ethnic groups.

Table 6.8   Commitment to the business: work versus other activities

			percentage of each ethnic group
	Indian	African Asian	Pakistani	All South Asians
I do the best I can in business even if it interferes with the rest of my life				
Agree strongly	15	33	27	25
Agree a little	49	31	27	36
Neither	15	19	15	16
Disagree a little	4	6	9	6
Disagree strongly	15	8	15	13
Can't say	2	3	6	3
Unweighted base	*53*	*36*	*33*	*129*

Table 6.9   Reasons for not planning to expand

			percentage of each ethnic group
	Indian	African Asian	Pakistani	All South Asians
Too old	9	9	17	13
Would reduce time with family	21	14	17	18
Family don't need employment	3	0	0	1
Making sufficient money	15	14	9	13
Have enough money	15	9	4	10
Too much stress	48	36	57	48
Too much risk	6	32	35	21
Too many management problems	3	5	0	3
No family members to help	6	0	9	5
Would need to recruit	6	0	0	3
Other	27	36	26	29
Unweighted base	*33*	*22*	*23*	*80*

Among those not planning to expand a number gave personal (too old, 13 per cent) and family reasons (would reduce time with the family, 18 per cent; family did not need jobs, 1 per cent) (Table 6.9). Some felt they had no monetary need to expand. However, most reasons for not expanding related to the business difficulties expansion would bring: stress (48 per cent), risk (21 per cent) and, for much smaller proportions, recruitment and management problems. Rather surprisingly, few Indians gave risk as a reason not to expand (6 per cent compared with about one third of Pakistanis and African Asians), while stress was more of an issue among Pakistanis than African Asians, with Indians falling between the two.

In the long term, most respondents wanted to retire (64 per cent) rather than always continue in business (17 per cent), although a large proportion were unsure about this (19 per cent) (Table 6.10). There was remarkable similarity between ethnic groups.

Table 6.10   Commitment to the business: desire to retire

				percentage of each ethnic group
	Indian	African Asian	Pakistani	All South Asians
Prefer to retire in long term	63	65	64	64
Prefer to work in the business always	18	15	18	17
Don't know	20	21	18	19
Unweighted base	*51*	*34*	*33*	*124*

However, about one third were reluctant to give up involvement in their business when they retired (Table 6.11). More Indians wanted a continuing role. Those who wanted to continue to have a role either expected to give advice without control (14 per cent) or retain control (14 per cent). The role expected by African Asians was more often one of adviser than controller, compared with the other two main groups.

Table 6.11   Role in business post-retirement

	Indian	African Asian	Pakistani	All South Asians
			percentage of each ethnic group	
Planning to have a role	40	27	30	33
Nature of role				
Give advice without control	15	21	9	14
Retain control	19	3	18	14
Contribute capital	0	6	3	2
Retain part/whole ownership	4	3	6	5
Other	2	3	0	2
Unweighted base	*52*	*34*	*33*	*125*

A further way in which the study examined views about the business was to investigate the extent to which the self-employed saw their business as offering appropriate employment for a son. Respondents were asked to rank the first three most important factors which they would want their son's first job to offer and then were asked if their business offered these (Tables 6.12 and 6.13).

The factors selected as important were interesting indicators of values. Security figured high among first choices, as did starting pay. The high priority given to job security speaks volumes about the insecurity of employment involved in small-scale self-employment. Once second and third choices were added, advancement was important to a large proportion and interest and working conditions to a large minority. There were major differences across ethnic groups. Whilst advancement and security were important across all three groups, Pakistanis were much more concerned about deriving respect through the job, Indians focused more on starting pay and security, African Asian respondents were more diverse. Both African Asians and Indians were more concerned about interest and working conditions than were Pakistanis. On the other hand, African Asians lay between Indians and Pakistanis in their focus on extrinsic rewards, being closer to

Pakistanis in respect of seeing good starting pay as important and closer to Indians in the proportion who saw respect as important.

Table 6.12   Three most important factors in a first job

	Indian	African Asian	Pakistani	All South Asians
			percentage of each ethnic group	
Secure job for the future	60 (41)	63 (34)	69 (28)	63 (35)
Good starting pay	65 (46)	38 (28)	45 (24)	49 (33)
Opportunities for promotion	54 (0)	69 (13)	66 (3)	62 (5)
Interesting work	52 (13)	56 (19)	17 (3)	45 (12)
Good working conditions	58 (0)	47 (3)	28 (3)	46 (2)
Job respected by people in general	10 (0)	22 (0)	66 (34)	29 (10)
Unweighted base	*48*	*32*	*29*	*114*

Figures in brackets give the most important factor.

Over one quarter felt their business could not provide those factors which they felt were important, while only 15 per cent felt their business could completely provide those factors. Pakistanis were much less likely than other groups to feel their business could provide these factors, with 58 per cent saying their business could not, compared with 15 per cent of Indians and 16 per cent of African Asians. Whilst the high proportion of Pakistanis who thought their business did not provide those factors important for a son may partly be a reflection of the limited nature of those businesses, nevertheless, the fact that only 15 per cent of all the Asians could unreservedly recommend their own business as a suitable job for their son is significant. It suggests that the migrant generation were willing to do work that they do not think is good enough for their children, and that their economic aspirations for their children are higher than those for themselves.

Table 6.13 Business provides factors for son's job

	Indian	African Asian	Pakistani	All South Asians
			percentage of each ethnic group	

Whether their business could provide the three factors identified in Table 7.13

	Indian	African Asian	Pakistani	All South Asians
Yes, completely	15	16	16	15
Yes, partly	28	34	7	23
Yes, a little	4	0	10	7
No	15	16	58	27
Can't say	38	34	10	27
Unweighted base	*47*	*32*	*31*	*117*

Given these views, it was important to see whether respondents did intend their children to take over their business. Nearly all respondents had a child, usually more than one, and three-quarters of Pakistanis had more than three children. About half of the self-employed did not want any of their children to take over their business, whilst about one fifth did (Table 6.14). The remainder were unsure. Indians in particular (40 per cent) and African Asians (27 per cent) were more likely to be unsure whether they wanted a child to take over the business, whereas almost all Pakistanis knew they definitely did or did not want a child to take over the business. Almost one third of Pakistanis did want a child to take over, compared with one sixth of Indians and African Asians. At the same time 62 per cent of Pakistanis did not want their children to take over, compared with 57 per cent of African Asians and 44 per cent of Indians.

This is quite a remarkable finding, and both economic and cultural factors seem to be at work. As we have seen, Pakistanis seemed to rate less highly the benefits of their business to their children. The businesses were also less economically successful. It was therefore not surprising that more Pakistanis than other groups did not want their children to take over. However, more also wanted their children to take over and this seemed to result from a higher proportion having views about what they wanted their children to do than did Indians and, to a lesser extent African Asians.

Table 6.14   Children to take over the business

	Indian	African Asian	Pakistani	All South Asians
percentage of each ethnic group				
Whether respondent wants their children to take over the business				
Yes	17	17	31	21
Don't know	40	27	7	27
No	44	57	62	52
Unweighted base	48	30	29	111

Base: those who were currently in business and had children.

What is perhaps most evident in the fact that half the sample did not want any of their children to take over their business are rising expectations, or at least rising aspirations. Our finding can be contrasted with the finding of Aldrich et al in the late 1970s that while only a quarter of white self-employed wished their children to inherit their business, half the Asians did (see Table 1.1 in Chapter 1). It seems that parents are not content for their children to do the same work as they have done. This may at least be partly attributable to migration, as migrants are often willing or forced to take on low paid, low status, marginal work with long hours in order to get themselves established, but then expect their children to enter higher paid, higher status work. This is particularly likely to be the case where migration resulted in downward social mobility and migrants have spent their working lives trying to reverse the process and wish to see their children restored to the family's pre-migration social status. There is some reason to think that this is what has been happening in the case of South Asians in Britain.

It is sometimes asserted that migrants 'have tended to be from the poorest and most underprivileged groups of their countries of origin' (Anthias and Yuval-Davis, 1992:77). This is almost certainly not the case. An analysis of 1972 data from the Nuffield Social Mobility Survey found that nearly a quarter of the nonwhite migrants had professional class origins, predominantly higher professional, which was twice the proportion of the native English; and over half had social origins in either the petty bourgeoisie or the farming classes (the figure for the English was 16 per cent) (Heath and Ridge, 1983). The analysis shows that on migration there was, however, a serious downward social mobility as people of professional origins failed to secure professional posts, and the petty bourgeoisie was 'proletarianised': children of self-employed traders, artisans and farmers met the demand for labour in British factories (Heath and Ridge, 1983).

An earlier PSI study, too, found that the initial effect of migration was downward social mobility as the overwhelming majority of migrants could only get manual work, including persons with academic qualifications, even degrees, and who may have been in white-collar work before migration (Smith, 1977). The initial downward mobility was accepted because it still offered much higher earnings than available in the countries of origin, but it is not surprising that those individuals who have been able to resist-gradually the proletarian character ascribed to migrant labour and their families should have endeavoured to do so. Self-employment may itself have been a part of this process; but for some it may have been a stage in this process, rather than a goal.

Whether the goal of higher occupational status for their children than self-employment offers will be achieved cannot be answered with any certainty. Two things ought to be noted however. A study of white shopkeepers has shown that in terms of social mobility, self-employment offers an intergenerational 'springboard': the children of shopkeepers are disproportionately likely to succeed in joining prestigious professions (Bland, Elliot and Bechhofer, 1978). Secondly, while there is continuing evidence of racial bias in the labour market, so that ethnic minorities have to be better qualified than whites in order to achieve the same job-levels (Heath and McMahon, 1995), African Asians and Indians (but not Pakistanis) are producing more higher qualified persons than whites (Modood et al, 1997). In this study too we found that the children of the self-employed, especially the

Indians and African Asians, had very high levels of participation in post-16 education (Table 2.13), and (including the Pakistanis) had achieved high levels of attainment, with a half of all aged 18 or over having acquired at least one A level or equivalent qualification (Table 2.14). The result is decreasing racial disadvantage in the labour market, and, in fact, African Asians have probably achieved parity with whites (Jones, 1993; Iganski and Payne, 1996). We do not have enough evidence to evaluate the extent self-employment has played a part in this, but the blocked mobility thesis of earlier decades, one of the sources of Asian self-employment, can no longer be said to apply to the same degree.

The self-employed, then, show considerable commitment to their business, with six out of ten putting it above the rest of their life, a quarter strongly so, with a third not certain that they wanted to retire from it, and another third intending to maintain their involvement after retirement. Yet only a sixth thought that their business could completely provide what their son should be looking for in his first job, and less than half thought it provided these factors at all. In fact half the sample did not want any of their children to take over the business compared to a fifth who did. It seems that the commitment of the self-employed to their business is considerable but instrumental: it is to provide current income and serve the family rather than to raise children to serve the business. This suggests that the emergence of Asian self-employment must be seen in the context of an Asian commitment to the family and to strategies to improve the prospects of the family, especially the next generation.

SUMMARY AND CONCLUSION

Asian self-employment has been seen as an 'economic dead end' by some commentators (Aldrich et al, 1981). The evidence from this and the previous chapter gives mixed support to this view. About half saw turnover growing and three-quarters saw their income as at least at medium level, which other evidence suggests is on average higher in self-employment than in another job. Moreover, nearly 10 per cent of the businesses together employed

273 people, and 8 per cent of the sample owned more than one business. At the same time, one fifth had had declining turnover and only 7 per cent regarded their income as high, the incomes of Pakistanis was particularly low, and 42 per cent of the businesses were without employees. We should also not forget that the sample excludes nearly all of those who had left self-employment (other than those who had left in the previous year), including those who failed in business.

However, more important, the evidence suggests that the purpose of self-employment and the achievement in self-employment should not be seen in such narrow, economic terms:

- most of the self-employed derived feelings of self-worth and status from their business;

- many derived feelings of moral or religious satisfaction;

- many found interest and derived independence from their business;

- businesses strengthened family cohesion and allowed the owner to provide employment for their family.

On the negative side, hours were one of the drawbacks of self-employment. Most worked long hours and most wanted to work fewer.

The degree to which self-employment was not a 'dead end' depended not only on measures of achievement but on whether those factors mattered to the individual. Here, perhaps more than anywhere, economic and cultural factors interplayed: economic factors often created the outcome; cultural factors whether the outcome was valued and what level of outcome was seen as successful.

Not surprisingly, given the lower rate of economic success of Pakistani businesses, this group was more likely to report a low income and that they had some problems managing financially. In fact, almost half regarded their income to be low compared with very few from the other two groups. However, difficulties managing financially were only uncommon for Indians, while African Asians seemed to worry about money more often.

In terms of identity and self-worth, Pakistanis less often felt they achieved status through their business and more often wanted it. In part this may have been due to lower economic success; in part to their greater concern to achieve status and respect through the business. Indians, who seemed least concerned about gaining status, were also fairly unlikely to report gaining it. The starkest difference appeared in relation to status within the family and it appeared that, whilst this was important to Pakistanis and self-employment was a means to gaining status, this link was less strong among Indians.

Although moral and religious achievement seemed to be expressed differently by Indians and African Asians on the one hand and Pakistanis on the other, many seemed to derive such benefits. However, the achievement was strongest for Pakistanis and African Asians, to whom religion was often more important compared with Indians.

Unfortunately the same pattern was not found in the achievement of independence. Independence had been a motivating factor in becoming self-employed for Pakistanis more than for other groups, but it is clear that not all had achieved this aim. For the other groups, a much higher proportion found independence than sought it. Similarly, Indians, who set more store on leisure, tended to work the longest hours and more were dissatisfied in this respect.

Thus, with a wider definition of success in self-employment, it can be seen that business brought success across ethnic groups. However, the link between economic success and success in other terms seemed to be strong, resulting in Pakistanis tending to be somewhat less successful, despite differences in cultural values of success.

The experience of running one's own business seemed to have lessened drive, with fewer wishing to expand, with other needs becoming more prominent (avoidance of stress and risk and desire to spend time with the family). Despite less dynamism, many were still committed to running the business, with many preferring either never to retire or to maintain a role in the business once retired.

However, such commitment seemed to be confined to their own role, rather than commitment to the business, as half did not want their children to take the business over. It seems that business was good enough for them but not for their children. The difference between groups may reflect a difference in commitment to business (and its various benefits) and the role of the parent. More probably it reflects the qualification levels and the perceived career opportunities available for their children. Thus the greater number of Pakistanis who wanted their children to take over the business suggests that they are more likely to perceive the next generation as suffering from a similar lack of opportunities as they themselves. This is consistent with what is generally known about the qualification levels and the occupational mobility that the new generation of African Asians and Indians are achieving.

Self-employment may have played an important role in mitigating the downward occupational mobility experienced by South Asians on entry into Britain and the high rates of unemployment from the start of the recession in the mid-1970s. There is no evidence that self-employment was the prospect with which migrants came to Britain. Rather, it seems to have been a strategy that utilised the resources of South Asians, within different community norms and appreciation of status, in the context of poor employment prospects, aggravated by racial discrimination. As these factors change, so the attractiveness of self-employment, especially for the second generation, may change. It may be, therefore, that self-employment, for at least some Asian groups will turn out to be only a temporary stage in pursuit of the migrants' goal – economic betterment for themselves and their families.

If the upward occupational mobility (or perhaps more accurately, the reversal of a previous downward mobility) that the self-employed wish for their children is achieved, there will be a sense in which the 'economic dead-end thesis' will have been proved true and false. True because self-employment as an economic force will lose momentum; false because self-employment will have contributed to providing the springboard for the next generation. This is, at this stage, somewhat speculative, but it is worth drawing out an important implication. If it should indeed prove to be the case that up to half the children of the existing Asian self-employed do not enter their parents' small businesses, then after two decades of remarkable growth, we could begin to see a decline in the rate of self-employment among at least some South Asian groups. There is some evidence that some South Asian groups are becoming well-represented at the level of middle and big businesses (for example, 12 businesses in our sample of 129 together employed 273 persons). It cannot, however, be taken for granted that the current high rates of participation in small-scale self-employment will be indefinitely sustained for all Asian groups. Some have assumed that the current high levels in rates of self-employment combined with a youthful age-structure mean a continuing trend of high rates of self-employment (Ward, 1991). But existing South Asian self-employment has been a result of particular kinds of interactions between opportunity structures and cultures; to the extent that either of these elements changes, it will affect the character and scale of South Asian self-employment.

Chapter 7

Conclusions: The Interaction of Culture and Economics

Against the background of a rapid growth in Asian self-employment over the last two decades, this research sought to help explain the diversity between South Asian groups in Britain in the extent of self-employment and in the size of businesses. Previous research into ethnicity and self-employment has provided economic and cultural explanations of the nature of self-employment among ethnic minorities. Aldrich et al (1981), Jones et al (1994) and Ram (1992) found that one of the major explanations of Asian entry into self-employment was the desire to avoid racial discrimination and the resulting confinement to low-status jobs in the labour market. Others (Werbner, 1990a and 1990b; Srinivasan, 1992 and 1995) have identified cultural traits as potentially predisposing South Asian entry into business and ultimately explaining its success. Waldinger et al (1990) have suggested an approach which combines the economic with ethnicity perspectives. Their interactive approach is built on two dimensions: opportunity structures and characteristics of the ethnic group. While this is a theoretical advance, it does not take the idea of 'interaction' far enough. It still assumes that 'opportunity structures' can be culturally neutral and can be defined independently of ethnic group norms and attitudes – an assumption challenged by our study.

In particular, we wished, firstly, to understand better the relative influence of cultural and economic factors on self-employment. This involved examining to what extent self-employment is a positive choice, seen as offering benefits (economic, psychological and social), and to what extent it is a result of labour market difficulties and racial discrimination; how economic, social and religious factors affect the nature of self-employment and outcomes; and how familial roles encourage and facilitate self-employment. Secondly, we wished to examine to what degree self-employment is a vehicle for employment not only for the self-employed themselves but also for others as employees and family workers. Thirdly, we wished to explore the extent to which self-employment provides upward mobility, where upward mobility is defined in terms of the respondents' aspirations as well as in terms of income, occupational status and social status.

The research aimed to contribute to discussions about inequalities in Britain and what degree of upward socio-economic mobility is possible, especially for groups who suffer racial discrimination. Specifically, we sought to contribute to the improvement of the knowledge base for the development of employment policies aimed at lessening racial disadvantage and promoting opportunities for ethnic minorities.

THE INFLUENCE OF CULTURAL AND ECONOMIC FACTORS ON SELF-EMPLOYMENT

There was extensive evidence of differences in cultural and economic factors affecting self-employment: in entry into self-employment, development of the business and satisfaction with self-employment. While this was manifest in differences in self-employment between the three ethnic groups (Indians, African Asians and Pakistanis), it also showed in differences in the homogeneity within ethnic groups.

Self-employed Indians and Pakistanis formed two fairly homogeneous groups, with similarities within each group of experience in business. African Asians were more heterogeneous, with the group exhibiting bipolar experiences (for example, high proportions doing well or badly in business). Part of the explanation seemed to lie in the greater educational homogeneity of Indians and Pakistanis compared with African Asians, who tended to be

either unqualified or highly qualified. The more mixed characteristics of African Asian businesses may also have been related to
this group's greater religious diversity, compared with Indians,
nearly all of whom were Hindus or Sikhs, groups who in terms of
cultural adaptation are similar to each other (Modood, Beishon
and Virdee, 1994; Modood et al, 1997), and compared with
Pakistanis, all of whom were Muslims.

Both economic and cultural factors were important motiva-
tors for going into business. As in other studies we found the
movement into self-employment was not usually from unemployment. Pakistanis, however, appeared to suffer more from poor
employment prospects and racism at work. These reasons for
going into business were put forward by the majority. A substantial minority of African Asians suffered the same problems,
although satisfaction with pay prospects and skill development
prior to self-employment was high in this group. These push factors interacted with rather different pull factors for each group.
Pakistanis and African Asians tended to see running a business as
conferring status with their family (and, to a lesser degree, with
others), whereas Indians seemed to attach more importance to
the possibility of increasing their income and the degree of self-
determination that being their own boss conferred. Thus, while
all groups exhibited both push and pull factors, Indians, to the
greatest extent, appeared to be making positive choices to enter
business; Pakistanis and, to a lesser extent, African Asians were
using self-employment as an escape from racism and poor
employment prospects. At the same time, in cultural terms,
Indians stressed individualism and income, whist Pakistanis and
African Asians stressed status, especially with the family, indicating either that status was more important to these two groups or
that self-employment was identified with status for these groups.
However, for Pakistanis, employment and income problems prior
to self-employment may have resulted in self-employment being
seen to confer status.

Complementing entry into self-employment for positive reasons, Indians seemed to have better access to capital, with few
experiencing problems in this area. As well as using savings, more
Indians than other groups used institutional loans to finance their
business. Given the need for entrepreneurs to draw up business

plans and, often, to offer security for bank loans, this suggested Indians had greater initial wealth, combined with a business orientation. Over one third of Indians entered self-employment by taking over an existing business, a less risky approach than starting from scratch, but this may have increased the need for and capacity to get loans. Most Indians (59 per cent) ran retail or catering businesses, particularly small groceries/off licences and newsagents, although one sixth each were in artisan-based services and in other services. Indian businesses were least likely to be single-person concerns and generally had more employees (paid or unpaid). African Asians required fewest loans but also seemed to have least access to finance, with over one third reporting problems in this area. They tended to have to rely on savings rather than bank loans. This group was more oriented towards developing business around pre-existing skills, and this was reflected in the line of business, with one third running artisan-based businesses. Retail and catering figured least for this group, although still accounting for 41 per cent of businesses.

Nearly all Pakistanis established their business from scratch, tending to rely on a single source of finance, most frequently their own savings. This may be partly explained by Muslim conceptions of economic justice and disapproval of at least some kinds of interest-based loans, and also by the finding that bank managers and others may have negative stereotypes of Muslim entrepreneurs in comparison with Sikhs or Hindus (Deakins, Hussain and Ram, 1994). Half went into retail and catering, with a further quarter running taxicab businesses. Few went into manufacturing/construction. Religion may have influenced the choice of business for some, as, for two-thirds of Pakistanis and one quarter of African Asians, religion influenced the goods and services provided. It may also have constrained business development for some Pakistanis. For once a line of business had been entered into, the handling of alcohol was not a constraint for Indians and African Asians, but over 80 per cent of all Pakistani businesses for whom the handling of alcohol was relevant to their business did not handle it due to their religion.

Community and family support were important in many ways, through encouraging self-employment, helping with finance and providing assistance in the business (paid or unpaid). More than half the respondents did in fact have a family history of self-employment, though few had worked in a family business. About one fifth may have benefited, through having relatives in the same line of business, from access to knowledge specific to the business they themselves would eventually own, and the high proportion with relatives in business at all encouraged or assisted self-employment. The family was clearly important to the respondents. Between two-thirds and three-quarters in each group said that what was best for their family took precedence over their own personal well-being.

We found no evidence of the moral individualism that some say characterises the self-employed (see, for example, Bechhofer et al, 1974; though see Hakim, 1988). Indeed, the data were suggestive of the benefits of the intangible social capital formed by family ties of mutual obligation and trust, and of its spillover into more tangible contributions by family members (Sanders and Nee, 1996). Family members provided a source of labour for many businesses, with one third using only family workers in the business initially. Community and family financial support was more important for Indians and African Asians than Pakistanis. Indians, too, tended to enter self-employment as a joint enterprise with one or more partners and were more likely to have members of the family working in the business. This was partly because Indian women were more likely to be self-employed than other women, and Indian men mainly approved of married women working outside the home (in the family business or elsewhere). Pakistani men were divided on whether married women could do non-domestic work, and this might have acted as a constraint on the start-up costs and development of some Pakistani businesses. While very few respondents said they did not trust British people, the highest levels of trust were expressed for family members, followed by people from one's own religious (rather than ethnic) group. At the same time, desire for increasing one's status within the family was linked with running a business, particularly for Pakistanis and African Asians and this will have reinforced the intention to enter business.

The differences in the type of business and finance seemed to reflect not only differences in educational levels and in financial resources across the groups, but also differences in orientation towards self-employment and in family support. Indians, with a concentration of medium-level qualifications and better access to capital, seemed to exhibit a strong business orientation. African Asians combined business orientation with experience in the relevant lines of business and appropriate technical skills. Pakistanis, however, seemed to suffer from both financial and skill constraints, and demonstrated little business orientation, perhaps unsurprisingly, given the extent to which this group seemed to enter self-employment as an escape and as a way of gaining standing within the family. Even though Pakistanis and Indians were concentrated in fewer lines of business than African-Asians, the latter seem to have been better prepared for the line of business they entered. Despite these differences, on becoming self-employed just over one half of each group aimed to expand their business, mainly to increase income, although a quarter aimed to expand to increase their status.

As well as the link between business and family status, other cultural differences were apparent between Indians, Pakistanis and African Asians, which were likely to have influenced the approach to business. Indians appeared to be more risk averse, cautious and conservative (like the Edinburgh shopkeepers in Bechhofer et al, 1974); African Asians, while generally risk averse, were more welcoming to new ideas; and Pakistanis were most welcoming to new ideas and also least risk averse and cautious. Religious beliefs may have played a part in these attitudes. Nearly all Pakistanis said religion was very important to how they led their lives, compared to less than a third of Indians and African Asians, a finding supported by the large samples studied in the Fourth Survey. Moreover, nearly all Pakistanis said that the success of a business was largely dependent upon the will of God compared to two-thirds of Indians and less than half of African Asians. It may be that individuals who believe that their success or failure is dependent upon divine providence have less reason to be cautious. Differences between these groups on attitudes to risk-taking and innovation were despite the fact that Indians and African Asians displayed less conservative views than Pakistanis on gender roles (for more on the cultural conservatism of Pakistanis see Modood, Beishon and Virdee, 1994; Modood et al, 1997). Contemporary society has been described as a time of uncertainty so that for individuals to flourish they need to embrace uncertainty. The risk-taking Pakistanis in this study, however, seemed to be born of a mixture of economic insecurity and religious faith, with the latter providing a sense of security from which risk could be faced. These Muslims, and perhaps some of the other Asians too, can be compared to the early Protestants, who developed an entrepreneurial ethic based upon the ideas of predestination and that God will look after those who are God-fearing but economically aspiring.

The approach to and circumstances of business entry should strongly influence later development, with the more business-like orientations, better initial funding and so forth likely to result in greater success. To some extent this was apparent, with Pakistani businesses being least successful in terms of growth in turnover. Very few Indian businesses declined, although Indian businesses did not have the highest proportion growing; this pattern should be expected from the cautious and conservative approach described earlier. African Asian businesses were most likely to grow but almost as likely as Pakistani businesses to decline. It was unclear if this pattern was due to the heterogeneity of this group or because of the propensity of this group to enter businesses related to their skills rather than business considerations, resulting in greater fluctuations due to chance. At the same time, Indians appeared to be continuing their business-orientation through making greater change as entrepreneurs: just as Indians were more likely to buy existing businesses to enter into self-employment, so too they were more likely to sell their original business and buy another. Only 6 per cent of the sample had ceased being self-employed in the previous year, and none had ever gone bankrupt.

SELF-EMPLOYMENT AS A VEHICLE FOR EMPLOYMENT

An important issue is the extent to which South Asian businesses were developing to provide a new source of employment and the extent to which such businesses relied on or sought to provide family employment. As businesses developed, they increasingly became a vehicle for providing work for people, whether as employees or as unpaid family workers. From initially employing (paid or unpaid) 362 people, employment had grown to 576 by the time of the survey, that is by 60 per cent (or, including the respondents themselves, from 491 to 699, by 42 per cent). This was mainly accounted for by an increase in the number of businesses employing more than five people; there was no change in the proportion of single person businesses. Taking into consideration the long period of operation of many of the businesses, and that our methodology did not allow us to identify businesses that had failed before the Fourth Survey, self-employment cannot be seen as a source of employment sufficient for a majority of an ethnic group. Most Asian self-employment is not capable of creating much employment other than for the owner. There was some evidence, however, that the largest 10 per cent of the businesses have generated considerable employment, and 6 per cent of the sample had come to own two businesses, with 2 per cent owning three.

Indian businesses provided both more family and non-family employment, both initial and through their development. Despite the larger number of non-family employees, Indian businesses, more than Pakistani and African Asian, can be characterised as family concerns, both being jointly run and employing family members. The employment potential of African Asian businesses was lowest: businesses were often sole ventures and rarely employed non-family members. Pakistani businesses started similarly to Asian African, with many owners working alone, although Pakistanis were more likely to employ non-family than family. However, they showed most developmental change, increasing employment provision, particularly in providing work for family.

While business growth was the main driving factor behind employment growth, there was evidence of the business being used to provide employment for the family. Avoiding unemployment was a factor in employing family workers particularly for Pakistanis, although all groups were equally influenced by the lack of decent employment opportunities. The business was also used explicitly as a vehicle for family cohesion, predominantly among Indians and African Asians. However, economic factors also entered the picture, with inability to afford others entering the picture as well as (mainly for Indians and African Asians) preferring family workers for their quality. Overall, the number of family workers increased from 92 to 145, with a slightly smaller increase in Indian-owned businesses. The proportion employing family members, however, was unchanged for Indians and African Asians, but increased from 39 per cent to 55 per cent for Pakistanis. The contrast between Indian businesses being jointly run and employing family members, and Pakistani businesses, despite probably being smaller, being less likely to employ family members, may be partly due to the differences in attitudes to working women held by these groups. The growth in family employees in the Pakistani businesses may be due to children coming of an age where they can help, as well as to the needs of the business.

SELF-EMPLOYMENT AS A VEHICLE FOR UPWARD MOBILITY: SUCCESS AND SATISFACTION

Measures of upward mobility are culturally based, dependent on the factors which different cultures attribute as important. Srinivasan, for example, has argued that Asian shopkeepers are motivated by the desire for status, but the status in question is not that of the white British but has its own criteria and rankings (Srinivasan, 1995). Hence we examined upward mobility not primarily in terms of income and occupation change, but of people's views of their success in business and in terms of a number of measures of satisfaction. We were also mindful of the difficulty found in the Fourth Survey in eliciting information on income. Thus the study examined success and benefits in a number of terms, including self-worth, independence and satisfaction, as well as finance. Because of the difficulties of getting information on levels of income, respondents were asked to rate their income on a scale of very high to very low. While this did not give information about the level, it did have the benefit of suggesting satisfaction with income.

Overall, most South Asian self-employed felt they had been successful in business. Not surprisingly, given the worse performance in terms of turnover, Pakistanis were least likely to feel they had been successful. This was also seen in terms of views about income. Over two-thirds felt that their income was at a medium level. While Indians and African-Asians exhibited similar patterns, with few considering their income low, nearly half of Pakistanis felt their income was low. This tallies with the reports of earnings given in the Fourth Survey. This indicates that the economic dead-end thesis even if considered in purely financial terms, is too pessimistic in relation to the African Asians and Indians, though nearer the mark in relation to the Pakistanis.

Not surprisingly, a large minority of Pakistanis had financial problems and frequent money worries, whereas few Indians did. A large minority of African Asians, too, reported financial problems. Yet, Indians and Pakistanis were equally likely to save regularly, whereas African Asians were not. These differences cannot be explained in terms of differences in the importance of money across ethnic groups, as there were none. If one accepts that people's views on the level of their income bears a relationship to the income they find acceptable to live on, it is tempting to attribute some differences to culture. Indians' greater caution and risk aversion, combined with considering their income medium to high, may have resulted in higher levels of saving and, consequently, fewer money worries than African Asians, despite African Asians' similar views of their income level, but greater willingness to accept risk. The degree of individual responsibility may also play a part, with a higher proportion of African Asians taking greater personal responsibility for their success than other groups (20 per cent of African Asians said God's will had nothing to do with success, compared with virtually no Indians and Pakistanis). While this would lead one to expect fewer Pakistanis, almost all of whom attributed business success to God's will, having money worries, the perceived low level of their income would counteract this.

Business brought benefits in terms of feelings of self-worth: nearly all derived feelings of self-worth from their business and a high proportion felt the business gave them standing with their family. For two-thirds, business also gave standing with the wider community and British society. Differences across ethnic groups in the satisfaction sought from business and their achievement, suggested that Indians (who were less concerned about achieving standing through their business) and African Asians (who reported achieving standing through their business) successfully derived the benefits sought but that Pakistanis were less successful.

Business also conferred feelings of independence, an important benefit given that many had sought independence through self-employment. Although feelings of independence were high across all groups, this was less so for Indians. However, Indians were less likely to have sought independence through self-employment; as more Pakistanis had done so, Pakistanis must be seen as being less successful also in this respect. Different aspects of the nature of the business may have come into play here. Indians were more likely to work with their family and so be less independent than other groups, whereas the desire for independence among Pakistanis may have been promoted by the poor labour market conditions from which self-employment had appeared an escape. Nevertheless, given the number of indicators (less growth in turnover, lower profits, less personal satisfaction from the business and a desire to work longer hours), the high proportion of Pakistanis who did derive feelings of independence from their business was surprising and, probably, also due to their comparative position prior to self-employment.

Issues of control and satisfaction were also examined through the hours worked. Most respondents worked between 40 and 59 hours per week, with only 10 per cent working fewer hours and little variation across ethnic groups. Although most people wanted to work fewer hours, dissatisfaction with the number of hours was greatest among Indians. Although the longer hours of Indians offer an explanation for this, cultural and economic factors also appeared to be at work, with Indians placing a higher value on leisure than other groups, and most appearing to be reasonably satisfied with their level of income, that is to say dissatisfaction with income was less likely to be an impetus to work longer.

EXPLANATIONS OF DIFFERENCES IN THE PROFILE OF
SOUTH ASIANS IN SELF-EMPLOYMENT

The first objective of the study was to increase our understanding of business differences between South Asian groups, rather than variation in the proportion of each group of self-employed. The research shows that the interaction between economic and cultural factors varies for the three groups resulting in variation in business growth and success.

Many Pakistanis entered business as an escape (from poor employment prospects and racism in the labour market) rather than as a positive choice. The resources they brought in terms of finance and skills were poor. The decision to enter self-employment in these circumstances may have been reinforced by a religious approach which created a faith-derived optimism about the results of economic activity. Additionally, the Pakistanis placed value on self-employment as a means of improving standing with the family. Against this background, it is not surprising that Pakistani businesses tended to be less successful. Self-employment brought both satisfaction and problems, although the religious outlook may have reduced the stress this brought.

Indians appeared to have a greater business-orientation: self-employment was more often entered for positive reasons and entry and development seemed to take greater account of business opportunities. Both educationally and financially, Indians seemed able to call on resources (savings, commercial loans and family loans). Although perceptions of status were less likely to encourage entry into self-employment, family cohesion was a support, with Indians more often entering businesses with family partners. Indians' greater risk aversion may have affected both who set up in business and then how the business developed. Against a sounder initial background, this was likely to result in the greater stability (including lower decline) of Indian businesses.

African Asians were a more heterogeneous group in terms of qualifications and seemed to exhibit a mix of the circumstances and attitudes of both Pakistanis and Indians. A large minority escaped into self-employment, and cultural values on self-employment and family standing also pushed some into self-employment. They shared the business-orientation of Indians, but were more likely to develop business around their skills and less likely to buy existing businesses, perhaps because they did not appear to have good access to capital. This background meant that African Asian businesses were among those most likely to grow, but also among those most likely to decline.

While some 'pull' factors and some facilitating factors were present for each group, though in different degrees and combinations, this does not amount to a strong predisposition to self-employment as such among any of the three South Asian ethnic groups. Each group was well-represented with a family history of self-employment: self-employment was seen as a vehicle to increase standing with the family for African Asians and Pakistanis, and family resources and capital were forthcoming for Indian entrepreneurs. While this certainly makes self-employment viable and attractive for some Asians, the perception of viability and attractiveness depends upon what are the alternatives and how they are perceived. That self-employment has been attractive to Asians in Britain is connected to their marginality and exclusion from more mainstream opportunities. Poor labour market prospects and racism had played a major role in the decision of Pakistanis (and a lesser role in the decisions of African Asians) to enter business. As evidence suggests this is reducing (Iganski and Payne, 1996; Modood et al, 1997), the circumstances which originally precipitated greater self-employment among these groups seems to be waning. Existing South Asian self-employment has been a result of particular kinds of interactions between opportunity structures and cultures; to the extent that either of these elements changes, it will affect the character and scale of South Asian self-employment.

RELEVANCE TO THE BRITISH-BORN GENERATION

A major issue is whether the high incidence of self-employment among South Asian immigrants will continue among the British-born. The study had hoped to look at differences in attitudes between first and second generation immigrants, but the low proportion of British-born in the sample (and therefore in business) precluded firm conclusions.

While future self-employed need not come from the same families, the wishes of the current groups of entrepreneurs about inheritance of the business added to the idea that the very high levels of self-employment may be a passing phase. The migrant generation's employment expectations for themselves, and what they were willing to do, were very different to their aspirations for their children. They may have been willing to put family before self, and work over leisure, but few entrepreneurs felt that the business provided what they would wish for a son in his first job. Nevertheless, one fifth wanted their children to take over their business, whereas half did not want them to. Indians, in particular, were uncertain. Pakistanis had more definite views, with one third wanting a child to take over the business and about a third not wanting this. Parental wishes may or may not be fulfilled, but it cannot be assumed that the current high levels of self-employment combined with a youthful age-structure mean a continuing trend of high rates of self-employment. A study of white shopkeepers has shown that their children are disproportionately likely to succeed in joining prestigious professions (Bland, Elliot and Bechhofer, 1978) and this is what the South Asian migrants hope for at least some of their children. The qualification levels of the children do lend support to the thesis that self-employment acts as an intergenerational 'springboard' into the professions. The economic dead-end thesis may turn out to be false about self-employment not being able to contribute to upward socio-economic mobility, even while true that the future of Asians does not predominantly lie in self-employment.

FUTURE RESEARCH PRIORITIES

We believe that this study demonstrates the relevance of cultural factors to economic opportunities and constraints. It shows that what counts as an 'opportunity structure' is conditioned by cultural factors. Historical studies have demonstrated that the origins of market capitalism lie in religious and ideological values no less than in 'objective' opportunities or 'economic rationality' (Weber, 1930; Tawney, 1926). This interaction of culture and economics is no less true today. Values associated with religious background, cultural assumptions about the social status of a business owner and future aspirations for children are relvant to understanding the experiences of British Asians in self-employment, the routes followed by different British Asian minorities into self-employment and the routes that, in many cases, they then plan for their children to move out of it.

The study calls for further research in a number of directions.

A. The dataset provides a valuable database on the employment and business histories and attitudes of the South Asian self-employed. This could be used to explore certain issues in more depth, for example, the interplay between education or religion and attitudes. The data could be further explored using more sophisticated techniques – factor analysis to generate composite variables, cluster analysis to examine factors underlying groupings and logistic regression to separate individual from group characteristics.

B. Our sample did not allow us to investigate our topics in relation to South Asian women, nor the second generation. Studies are required which target these populations.

C. There has been a recent call, based upon a study of the much larger US datasets, for further research into inter-ethnic variation in cultural practices as part of the explanation for group differences in rates of self-employment (Sanders and Nee, 1996:246). The topics from our study that require further research seem to be:

- the role of religion in self-employment, especially in the light of our findings about Muslims;

- the tangible and intangible ways in which families support and are supported by self-employment;

- the contribution of self-employment to the economic advancement of the self-employed and their families, including facilitating the children's entry into professional and managerial jobs.

IMPLICATIONS FOR POLICY

Although self-employment was often entered for negative reasons, it often provided entrepreneurs with status and satisfaction. However, the success of the business and benefits to the individual were related to the nature of entry into self-employment. At the same time differences were apparent between ethnic groups. A number of important policy conclusions may be drawn from this.

The evidence on business success suggests the need to ameliorate labour market conditions pushing South Asians into self-employment (racism and poor labour market prospects), so that entry is based on positive reasons. While there is some evidence that self-employment contributes to the economic advancement of some groups, no group seems to be intrinsically predisposed to self-employment. The second generation may have quite different expectations and sources of family and community support to those of migrants.

Access to finance needs to be improved. Although one fifth experienced difficulties in raising finance to establish the business, few used loans through government/local authorities or enterprise agencies. Finding a guarantor for a loan was the most common problem. As problems were most acute for Pakistanis, assistance targeting this group and African Asians would be particularly beneficial. Lenders and other funders of enterprise need to be aware of Muslim reservations about interest, and need to consider the advantages of alternative forms of funding such as buying a stake in the business. Some banks have recently begun to offer equity investment to small businesses (Bank of England, 1996). Indeed, this may be a form of support for small businesses which has distinct advantages of its own. It would, for example, bring the funder into a closer business relationship with the self-employed, and it would decrease the pressure of repayment at a time of recession or when the business was struggling, for the repayments would be based upon the size of profits.

There is a need for greater education and advice to encourage a more business-oriented approach: for example focusing on market opportunities as well as skills, and developing business plans to improve access to commercial loans. South Asians have clearly shown considerable ingenuity and determination in creating economic opportunities, and in assisting each other, especially through families, but many Asians entered self-employment with what seem to be very limited business skills, business plans or an analysis of markets. Consequently, many businesses have remained small, at best providing a limited livelihood for the self-employed individual, in return for very long hours from the individual and help from family members, including children. Researchers may not be the best persons to advise on business orientation, but it does seem to us that many Asians have been drawn into saturated markets (such as the corner grocery shop) and are in need of targeted support and advice in making those decisions that enable their enterprise to meet its objectives more successfully.

Finally, it is important that all advice and support should not operate under an assumption that South Asians are a homogeneous group. This book has striven to show that the differences between Asians are as important as the similarities. It follows that appropriate public and private sector support must be sensitive to the differences between South Asians. This is partly a matter of recognising cultural differences and how those cultures shape business motivation and constraints. Perhaps even more important, it is a matter of recognising the very different educational-economic profiles of different groups; that the difficult situation of Pakistanis (and Bangladeshis, whom we were not able to include in this study) will be obscured in statistical and other generalisations about Asians. We would like to think that this study provides the basis for discussions for developing culturally-sensitive policies which are able to identify and target those most in need of assistance, while at the same time affording recognition of the contribution that Asian self-employment is making to the British economy and society.

Appendix

RESEARCH METHOD

The investigation of the interaction between culture, economics and self-employment is extremely challenging for research design. Complex issues, entailing multiple interactions, would usually be researched either through a large-scale survey or through in-depth case studies. A qualitative approach was indicated by the emphasis on exploring culture and also by the variety of experience (work and business histories) which respondents might have had. Work histories need not be a simple progression into self-employment, and attitudes and culture needed to be examined at a number of points in time, related to major employment transitions.[1] Moreover, some aspects of culture, such as interactions within groups (particular networks supporting self-employment), might be better explored taking an ethnographic approach.

These considerations suggested we should take a qualitative, and perhaps a longitudinal, approach within the study. However, we also wished to quantify differences across ethnic groups and we considered it important that, unlike most earlier studies, the research should not be geographically specific: we wanted to be able to abstract from general local economic factors. Therefore, a fairly large sample was needed. The cost of a large number of qualitative interviews was prohibitive, as was the integration of ethnographic studies over several areas.

In order to address these conflicting demands, an approach marrying qualitative and quantitative approaches was developed. A detailed structured questionnaire was designed, which enabled a complex picture to be built up of each respondent. The resulting information could then be analysed quantitatively and as individual case studies. This book is based on quantitative analysis of the data.

The research also had to tackle difficulties in relation to the conduct of research across cultures and across languages. Questions in structured questionnaires are devised to have very specific meanings. While researcher and respondent may not always attach the same meanings to questions and responses, differences in meaning are likely to be greater the greater the cultural divide between the two. This will be further exacerbated where research is designed in a different language to that commonly used by the respondent. To some extent these difficulties were reduced by the ethnic and cultural diversity of the research team. To reduce the scope for misinterpretation of questions, the questionnaire was translated into five Asian languages. Translations were checked by other translators and discussed with the researchers. These factors should help to reduce errors, but scope for differences in meaning and interpretation remain. In addition, to encourage accurate response on sensitive issues, interviewers and respondents were ethnically matched.

THE SAMPLE

Identification of the self-employed is a major problem for research in this area. Studies tend to use sampling frames of businesses, not people (that is to say self-employed), and equate self-employment with small business. This introduces a number of biases. In most cases, the self-employed owners of large businesses are excluded and, depending on the nature of the sampling frame, the self-employed person operating from home is underrepresented, as are those with businesses which do not advertise through the major directories.

The problem of bias was greatly reduced for this study because of access to the respondents from the Fourth National Survey of Ethnic Minorities, which had been conducted by the Policy Studies Institute and Social and Community Planning

Research in 1994. The Fourth National Survey was a representative, national survey of ethnic minorities which, along with other aspects of economic activity, identified self-employment. It could, therefore, provide a sampling frame of self-employed people directly, rather than via businesses.

We intended to use the Fourth National Survey as a sampling frame to provide an achieved sample of 150 self-employed South Asians, spread equally across the four main South Asian groups in Britain (Pakistanis, Bangladeshis, Indians and East African Asians). We also aimed to stratify the sample, as necessary, to enable analysis by gender and by immigrant/British-born. For reasons of cost, the survey was to be confined to six geographical areas.

At the initial design stage of this study, the self-employment data in the Fourth National Survey were not available. Once the data were available, some aspects of the sample design had to be revised. The main problem was the smallness of the sample frame, a problem which was most severe for Bangladeshi self-employed.[2] In addition, the sample of British born and of female self-employed was small.[3] Within six areas it was not possible to achieve a sample of 150, nor to balance the interviews across ethnic groups (let alone by country of birth or gender). These constraints led to increasing the number of areas to seven, selected to maximise the number of potential respondents and the number of Bangladeshis. The sample was also extended to include co-owners of the respondent's business. However, it was recognised that analysis would not be possible by gender nor immigrant status and that analysis by ethnic group would have to be confined to three groups (Pakistani, Indian and African Asian).

The survey was conducted in the following seven areas: London, Greater Manchester, the West Midlands, West Yorkshire (Bradford and Leeds only), Leicestershire (Leicester and Harborough only), Kent (Gravesham and Gillingham only) and Staffordshire (Stoke only). In these areas, the sample consisted of all self-employed respondents to the Fourth National Survey who had not said they were unwilling to participate in further surveys (the primary sample) and of co-owners (the secondary sample). At interview, respondents were asked for their agreement to interview any co-owners. Co-owners were then approached to participate. Table A.1 shows the distribution of the primary sample by area and ethnic group.

Table A.1   **Sample by ethnic group and location**

	Paki-stani	Bangla-deshi	Indian	African/Asian	Total
Area					
London	6	7	22	30	65
Greater Manchester	5	2	1	3	11
W Midlands	10	0	21	4	35
W Yorkshire	9	0	1	1	11
Leicestershire	0	0	4	9	13
Kent	2	1	6	2	11
Staffs	8	1	0	0	9
Total	40	11	55	49	155

Using this dual approach, 129 interviews were completed, with people who were self-employed at the time or had been within the previous year (that is those who had been self-employed at the time of the Fourth National Survey, but were no longer self-employed). Of the achieved sample, 53 were Indian, 36 were African Asian, 33 were Pakistani and seven were Bangladeshi. Owing to the size of the Bangladeshi sample, differences between Bangladeshis and other South Asian groups could not be examined. However, Bangladeshis are included (and shown separately) in all tables, as they were included in data referring to the whole sample. We would like to stress that this data should not be used to draw any conclusions about Bangladeshi self-employed in Britain. General characteristics of the sample are presented in Chapter 2.

THE SURVEY PROCEDURE AND THE QUESTIONNAIRE

The survey took place in the summer of 1995. The contact procedure, which differed between the primary and secondary samples was as follows. A letter, explaining the purpose of the survey was sent to all potential primary respondents (that is those who had participated in the Fourth Survey of Ethnic Minorities). The letter was sent in both English and in the language used for Fourth Survey interviews, if different. Ethnically-matched interviewers then made a visit. Interviewers were supplied with the questionnaire in English, with a translation into the South Asian language in which the Fourth Survey had been conducted, if other than English.

The questionnaire, which had been piloted, covered:

* *entry into self-employment – push factors:* particularly labour market experience prior to entering self-employment and views of that experience; cultural, religious and attitudinal orientation towards work;

* *entry into self-employment – pull factors:* orientation towards work and views on self-employment; market opportunity; cultural, religious and attitudinal factors encouraging self-employment;

* *entry into self-employment – facilitating factors:* access to capital; experience; contacts and advice; familiarity with self-employment, including family history of self-employment; support networks;

* *business achievement and expectations:* business growth; the definition of success: cultural attitudes towards responsibility and self-actualisation, money and status.

The questionnaire is much too long to be reproduced here. It has been deposited, together with the data-tape, at the ESRC Data Archive at the University of Essex.

Notes

1 In respect of entry into self-employment, the questionnaire needed to take into account, for example, that respondents might have more than one episode of self-employment punctuating periods of other types of

economic activity or inactivity; businesses might develop from part-time to full-time, with the individual initially being otherwise economically active (or not); individuals might run a number of businesses, either consecutively or concurrently. In respect of views and intentions, design needed to consider, for example, the intention to set up a business might have existed long before the business was started; the pattern of employment might be planned to progress to self-employment, it might inadvertently equip the individual for self-employment or might, through its poverty, thrust the individual into self-employment.

2   While the number of self-employed South Asians in the Fourth National Survey was not small (322), the main problem stemmed from a high proportion of the relevant sample (25 per cent of 317) who had said they were unwilling to be interviewed in any follow-up survey. For Bangladeshis, the problem was extreme, as the sampling frame contained only 17 self-employed people who were not unwilling to be re-interviewed.

3   Seventeen per cent of the self-employed in the Fourth National Survey were women and 15 per cent had been born in Britain or migrated under the age of five.

BIBLIOGRAPHY

Afshar, H (1989) 'Gender roles and the "moral economy of kin" among Pakistani women in West Yorkshire', *New Community,* 15(2) pp211-225

Aldrich, HE, JC Cater, TP Jones, and D McEvoy (1981) 'Business development and self-segregation: Asian enterprise in three British cities'. In C Peach, V Robinson and S Smith (eds) *Ethnic segregation in cities.* Croom Helm

Aldrich, H, TP Jones and D McEvoy (1984) 'Ethnic advantage and minority business development'. In R Ward and R Jenkins (eds) *Ethnic communities in business: strategies for economic survival.* Cambridge University Press

Anthias, F and N Yuval-Davis (1992) *Racialised Boundaries: Race, Nation, Gender, Colour and Class and the Anti-Racist Struggle.* Routledge

Bank of England (1996) *Finance for Small Firms. A Third Report.* Bank of England

Basu, A (1995) *Asian small businesses in Britain: an exploration of entrepreneurial activity.* University of Reading, Discussion Paper No 303, Series A, Vol VII

Baumann, Z (forthcoming, 1996) 'The Making and Unmaking of Strangers'. In P Werbner and T Modood (eds) *Debating Cultural Hybridity.* Zed Books

Bechhofer, F et al (1974) 'The Petits Bourgeois in the Class Structure: the Case of the Small Shopkeepers'. In F Parkin (ed) *The Social Analysis of Class Structure.* Tavistock Publications

Beck, U, A Giddens and S Lash (1994) *Reflexive Modernisation.* Polity Press

Bhachu, P (1986) *Twice Migrants.* Tavistock Publications

Blanchflower, D and A Oswald (1990) 'Self-Employment and the Enterprise Culture'. In R Jowell, S Witherspoon and L Brook (eds) *British Social Attitudes: the 7th report.* Gower

Bland, R, B Elliot and F Bechhofer (1978) 'Social Mobility in the Petite Bourgeoisie', *Acta Sociologica,* 21(3), pp229-248

Brown, C (1984) *Black and White Britain. The Third PSI Survey.* Policy Studies Institute

Burrows, R (ed) (1991) *Deciphering the Enterprise Culture: Entrepreneurship, Petty Capitalism and the Restructuring of Britain.* Routledge

Campbell, M and M Daly (1992) 'Self-employment: into the 1990s', *Employment Gazette,* June

Deakins, D, G Hussain and M Ram (1995) 'Ethnic Entrepreneurs and Commercial Banks: Untapped Potential', *Regional Studies,* 29(11), pp95-100

Giddens, A (1994) *Beyond Left and Right?* Polity Press

Hakim, C (1988) 'Self-employment in Britain: Recent Trends and Current Issues', *Work, Employment and Society,* 2(4), pp421-450

Hakim, C (1989) 'New recruits to self-employment in the 1980s', *Employment Gazette,* June

Heath, A and J Ridge (1983) 'Social Mobility of Ethnic Minorities', *Journal of Biosocial Science Suppl,* 8, pp169-184

Heath, A and D McMahon (1995) *Education and Occupational Attainments: the Impact of Ethnic Origins,* Paper 34, Centre for Research into Elections and Social Trends

Iganski, P and G Payne (1996) 'Declining Racial Disadvantage in the British Labour Market', *Ethnic and Racial Studies,* 19(1), Routledge

Jones, T (1993) *Britain's ethnic minorities.* Policy Studies Institute

Jones, T and D McEvoy (1991) *Ethnic resources and opportunity structure: Asian enterprise in Britain and Canada.* Paper presented to the round table on 'Entrepreneurs between two worlds'. Paris, December

Jones, TP, D McEvoy and G Barrett (1994) 'Labour intensive practices in the ethnic minority firm'. In J Atkinson and D Storey (eds) *Employment, the small firm and the labour market.* Routledge

Kuran, T (1995) 'Islamic Economics and the Islamic Subeconomy', *Journal of Econmomic Perspectives,* 9(4), pp155-173

McEvoy, D, TP Jones, J Cater and H Aldrich (1982) *Asian immigrant businesses in British cities.* Paper presented to the British Association for the Advancement of Science, Annual Meeting, September

Meager, N, G Court and J Moralee (1994) *Self-employment and the distribution of income.* Institute of Manpower Studies, Report 270, Brighton

Modood, T (1990) 'British Asian Muslims and the Rushdie Affair', *Political Quarterly,* 61(2), pp143-60; and in J Donald and A Rattansi (eds) *'Race', Culture and Difference.* Sage

Modood, T (1991) 'The Indian economic success: a challenge to some race relations assumptions', *Policy and Politics,* No.3, pp177-198; also in *Not Easy Being British: colour, culture and citizenship* (1992) Trentham Books; and in J Anderson and M Ricci (eds) (1994) *Society and Social Science: A Reader.* Second Edition. The Open University

Modood, T (1993) 'Muslims, Incitement to Hatred and the Law'. In J Horton (ed) *Liberalism, Multiculturalism and Toleration.* Macmillan

Modood, T (1996) 'The Changing Context of "Race" in Britain', Symposium on Anti-Racism in Britain, *Patterns of Prejudice,* 30(1), pp3-13

Modood, T, S Beishon and S Virdee (1994) *Changing Ethnic Identities.* Policy Studies Institute

Modood, T, R Berthoud, J Lakey, J Nazroo, P Smith, S Virdee and S Beishon (forthcoming 1997) *Ethnic Disadvantage in Britain.*

Owen, D (1993) *Ethnic minorities in Great Britain: economic characteristics.* 1991 Statistical Paper No 3. National Ethnic Minority Data Archive, University of Warwick

Peach, C (ed) (1996) *Ethnicity in the 1991 Census. Volume Two: The ethnic minority populations of Great Britain.* Office for National Statistics

Phizacklea, A (1990) *Unpacking the fashion industry.* Routledge and Kegan Paul

Rafiq, M (1992) 'Ethnicity and enterprise: a comparison of Muslim and non-Muslim owned Asian businesses in Britain', *New Community,* 19(1), pp43-60

Ram, M (1992) 'Coping with racism: Asian employers in the innercity', *Work, Employment and Society,* 6(4), pp601-618

Robinson, V (1990) 'Roots to mobility: the social mobility of Britain's black population, 1971-87', *Ethnic and Racial Studies,* 13(2)

Sanders, J and V Nee (1996) 'Immigrant Self-Employment: The Family as Social Capital and the Value of Human Capital', *American Sociological Review,* Vol 61, April, pp231-249

Scase, R and R Goffee (1981) 'Traditional Petty Bourgeois Attitudes: The Case of Self-Employed Craftsmen, *Sociological Review,* 19(4), pp729-44

Smith, DJ (1977) *Racial Disadvantage in Britain.* Penguin

Srinivasan, S (1992) 'The class position of the Asian petty bourgeoisie', *New Community,* 19(1), pp61-74

Srinivasan, S (1995) *The South Asian Petty Bourgeoisie in Britain.* Avebury

Tawney, R (1926) *Religion and the Rise of Capitalism: A Historical Study.* John Murray

Waldinger, R, H Aldrich, and R Ward (1990) *Ethnic entrepreneurs.* Sage

Ward, R (1987) 'Small retailers in inner urban areas'. In G Johnson (ed) *Business strategy and retailing.* John Wiley

Ward, R (1991) 'Economic Development and Ethnic Business'. In J Curran and R Blackburn (eds) *Paths of Enterprise: The Future of the Small Business.* Routledge

Watson, JL (ed) (1977) *Between Two Cultures: Migrants and Minorities in Britain.* Blackwell

Weber, M (1930) *The Protestant Ethnic and the Spirit of Capitalism* (tr. T Parsons). George Allen and Unwin

Werbner, P (1990a) *The Migration Process.* Berg

Werbner, P (1990b) 'Renewing an Industrial Past: British Pakistani entrepreneurship in Manchester', *Migration,* No 8, pp7-39